SAVING FAITH

How Does ROME Define It?

Saving Faith:

How does Rome
Define It?

William Webster

Is There a Basis for Unity
Between Roman Catholicism
and Evangelical Protestantism?

Christian Resources Inc.
1505 NW 4th Ave.
Battle Ground, WA 98604
(360) 687-7311
E-mail: WWebs84862@aol.com

*

©William Webster 1997

First Published 1995

ISBN 1-879737-27-2

Cover Design by Michael Rotolo

Quotations from *The Fundamentals of Catholic Dogma*, *The Question and Answer Catholic Catechism*, *The Code of Canon Law* and the *Documents of Vatican II* used by permission.

PRINTED IN THE UNITED STATES OF AMERICA

CONTENTS

⊫ 1 ⊫

THE CALL FOR UNITY: THE ECT ACCORDS

(Evangelicals and Catholics Together)

In March of 1994 the ECT Accord, spearheaded by Evangelical,Chuck Colson, and Roman Catholic, Richard John Neuhaus, was released to the public. And in November 1997, this ECT document was reformulated and released under the title, *The Gift of Salvation*, now popularly known as ECT 2. The efforts of those behind the Roman Catholic and Evangelical accords has generated a great deal of debate within both communions. Some have applauded these documents while others have taken a decidedly negative view towards them. In essence the documents call for the setting aside of doctrinal differences for the sake of unity in fighting against the encroaching darkness of secularism and humanism throughout the world. In light of the onslaught of such horrendous and ungodly behavior and activities as abortion, pornography, crime, drugs, immorality etc., it is suggested that it is high time that those who name the name of Christ should unite to bring Christian values to bear in a culture that is self destructing. While this has a certain appeal, the documents themselves and the concepts they endorse are seriously flawed.

The implicit assumption in the overall thrust of the documents is that the Evangelical and Roman Catholic

Churches teach and proclaim the same gospel and that the differences that separate them, while not unimportant, are nonetheless of secondary importance in view of the fundamentals of the gospel that they both supposedly affirm and embrace. This is the overall emphasis of articles recently carried by *Christianity Today* by J.I. Packer and Charles Colson defending their endorsement of ECT I. But when one looks to Colson and Packer for clarification of of the essentials of what it means to be a Christian, one cannot but be alarmed at their statements, especially of one the stature of Dr. Packer. In effect, they and the remaining signers of the document define a Christian as one who has embraced the fundamental doctrines as formulated by the major creeds and councils in the early church. As ECT 2 puts it:

> We give thanks to God that in recent years many Evangelicals and Catholics, ourselves among them, have been able to express a common faith in Christ and so to acknowledge one another as brothers and sisters in Christ. We confess together one God, the Father, the Son and the Holy Spirit; we confess Jesus Christ the Incarnate Son of God; we affirm the binding authority of Holy Scripture, God's inspired Word; and we acknowledge the Apostles' and Nicene creeds as faithful witnesses to that word.

Incredibly, there was no mention in the ECT 1 document that addressed the most important issue of all which was the focal point of the Reformation and the foundational truth of the gospel itself: justification by faith. This glaring omission was remedied somewhat in the newly released ECT 2 document in that justification by faith is emphasized but the document misrepresents the biblical and Reformation teaching on the subject as well as the true teaching of Rome. For example, the ECT 2 document makes the following statements regarding justification:

> Justification is central to the scriptural account of salvation,

and its meaning has been much debated between Protestants and Catholics. We agree that justification is not earned by any good works or merits of our own; it is entirely God's gift, conferred through the Father's sheer graciousness, out of love that He bears us in His Son, who suffered on our behalf and rose from the dead for our justification. Jesus was 'put to death for our trespasses and raised for our justification' (Rom 4:25). In justification, God, on the basis of Christ's righteousness alone, declares us to be no longer his rebellious enemies but his forgiven friends, and by virtue of his declaration it is so.

This statement is very misleading. It is misleading from both an Evangelical and Roman Catholic point of view. From an Evangelical perspective, this statement is an inaccurate description of justification. Justification is not the declaration that we are no longer God's enemies but his forgiven friends. It is the declaration, based on the *imputed* righteousness of Christ himself, that we are positively righteous before God and completely set free from the condemnation of the law and from any necessity for works for the attaining of the state of justification. While this declaration certainly leads to reconciliation with God and adoption into God's family, justification itself does not mean this in a biblical sense. But this statement is also muisleading from a Roman Catholic point of view. The Roman Catholic Church has officially condemned this teaching. To suggest that Rome agrees with the above statement that justification is not dependent in any way on human works and merit is a complete misrepresentation of its official position. As we will see in the documentation to follow, Rome clearly affirms the necessity for the works of sanctification as the basis for justification which merit eternal life. Just to anticipate this, note the following canon on Justification from the Council of Trent:

Canon XXIV. If any one saith, that the justice received is not preserved and also increased before God through good works; but that the said works are merely the fruits and signs of Justification obtained, but not a cause of the increase thereof: let him be anathema.

Rome has officially condemned the teaching that an individual is justified by the righteousness of Christ himself, alone imputed to the believer. In Roman Catholic theology works are indeed necessary and meritorious for justification and salvation.

While it is true that the Roman Catholic and Evangelical Churches share a common heritage of doctrine in the creeds and the doctrinal formulations of the early Councils, this does not mean that they share the same gospel. In his book, *Evangelical Catholics*, Keith Fournier (a Roman Catholic and promoter of ECT) expresses the theme of the book in this subtitle: *A Call for Christian Cooperation to Penetrate the Darkness with the Light of the Gospel*. This is a call for unity based on a supposed common foundation of the gospel. There is an implicit acknowledgment here that unity must be based on truth. But sadly, it is in the realm of the truth of the gospel that the Roman Catholic Church has erred. The creeds, as true as they are, are *not* the gospel.

And as one examines the official teachings of the Church of Rome it is clear that it does not teach the biblical gospel and that the Evangelical and Roman Catholic Churches are very divided on this issue. In fact, the Roman Catholic Church has *officially* repudiated the definition of a Christian as formulated by Keith Fournier and the signers of the ECT documents.

It is not without significance that men like Fournier and the signers of the ECT Accords studiously avoid clearly stating what the official salvation teachings of the Roman Catholic Church truly are. And sadly this is also true of the article by Packer in *Christianity Today*. But not only is there a purposeful avoidance of an honest and clear statement of Roman Catholic teaching, one finds in the writings of men like Fournier a misrepresentation of the true teachings of the

Church of Rome to make the institution appear virtually evangelical. There is a fundamemntal denial in some of his statements of doctrines dogmatically decreed by the Council of Trent, for example. An examination of those teachings, however, reveals that the Church of Rome has departed from the truth of the gospel. Thus, no unity is possible since we do not share the same basis of truth and therefore the same gospel. The Reformation was fought over issues of supreme importance which have direct bearing on the gospel. It will not do to minimize the doctrinal issues of the Reformation and suggest that they are somehow nothing more than a tragic misunderstanding over semantics. Interestingly, the Roman Catholic Church itself has never embraced that point of view. *It is only by repudiating the basic teachings of the Reformation as well as the authoritative teaching of the Roman Catholic Church itself that one can arrive at the attitude of those who have formulated the ECT documents.*

While it is true that Western culture is being inundated by humanism, secularism and sin of terrible dimensions, the call of the Scriptures is not simply to bring Christian values to bear in the culture but to proclaim the gospel. To be opposed to pornography and abortion, while certainly admirable and right, is not the defining standard of what it means to be a Christian or the focal point of the biblical mandate to the Church of Jesus Christ. There are undoubtedly many atheists, Jews, Mormons, Jehovah's Witnesses and others who are in genuine opposition to these particular behaviors and would stand with true Christians in fighting against them, but this does not mean that we are going to come together in unity downplaying the issues of theology. In the book of Galatians Paul anathematized a group of people known as the Judaizers who proclaimed a gospel that contradicted that which Paul had preached to the Galatians. It is important to note that these people did not deny the person of Christ. They were orthodox in their understanding of who Christ is and faithful in proclaiming this truth. Paul and these teachers shared a common heritage of truth that was fundamental to

Christianity. But their error lay in a denial the truth of justification by faith alone. They taught that in addition to the work of Christ one also had to add the works of the ceremonial and moral law as a grounds for salvation. There would not have been in Paul's mind any justification for the idea that in light of the terrible moral corruption of the Roman Empire, and given the common theological foundation that he and the Judaizers shared in that they both professed the person of Christ, that they should come together in a show of unity, laying aside their theological differences to fight the moral evils of the day. Paul would have none of this.

The ultimate issue in fighting the moral issues of the day is the proclamation of the gospel because it the gospel that is 'the power of God to salvation' (Rom. 1:16). We are not called to save the culture from moral decay, we are called to proclaim the gospel. And if we do not agree on the fundamentals of the gospel we cannot come together in unity. As one analyzes the teachings of Roman Catholicism it becomes clear that in principle the gospel that was proclaimed by the Judaizers which was placed under anathema by Paul is the gospel taught by the Roman Catholic Church, a gospel that denies in a fundamental sense justification by faith alone in Christ alone and which introduces human works and merit as an addition to the work of Christ. In effect, if the evangelical Church unites with the Church of Rome it will come together with an institution that proclaims a gospel that has been placed under an anathema by God Himself. It is out of concern to clarify these issues that I feel it is so important to clearly understand what the Roman Catholic Church officially teaches.

— 2 —

THE ROMAN TEACHING ON SAVING FAITH

The Roman Catholic Church teaches that justification is by grace through faith on account of Jesus Christ. This sounds quite orthodox, but on closer examination it becomes clear that the meaning of the terms faith, justification and grace are defined differently by the Roman Catholic Church from that of the Protestant. Though the two churches use the same terms they do not mean the same things by them. This is similar historically to the Pelagian controversy in the early 5th century. Pelagius was a heretic vigorously opposed by Augustine and the orthodox Church of his day. But both Pelagius and Augustine would have passed the test for unity as proscribed by the proponents of ECT 1 and 2. Both men affirmed the truth of the Apostles' and Nicene Creeds and the fourth century Councils. Was Augustine then wrong in opposing him? No, because his salvation teachings were indeed heretical. And yet Pelagius used orthodox theological terms in his teaching. He stated without qualification that he believed in salvation by grace through faith. But the problem is that the way he defined his terms contradicted their biblical and orthodox meaning. If one did not press Pelagius for definitions and was simply satisfied with general statements of

13

belief, then he would appear to be orthodox. Definition of terms is crucial because these words and what we say they mean must conform to their *biblical* meaning. It is of the utmost importance that we ask the question: What does the Roman Catholic Church mean by faith? What is the content of that faith and what precisely does it mean by justification? The Roman Church has not left us in doubt as to what it teaches about justification or faith and the doctrinal content of faith that is saving. By its dogmatic decrees as promulgated by Popes and ecumenical councils the Roman Catholic Church has clearly defined the meaning of such faith. We need to keep in mind that, in Roman Catholic theology, papal decrees when they are given *ex cathedra* are infallible as are the decrees of Ecumenical and Roman Catholic councils.

Thus, the decrees of the Council of Trent and Vatican I and the papal decrees on Mary form part of the doctrinal content of saving faith. These decrees are defined as being necessary to be believed for salvation and the Roman Church anathematizes all who would disagree with or reject these teachings.

We need to say a word here about the meaning of the term *anathema.* In the formal sense the term means excommunication from the Roman Catholic Church. However, the essential meaning of the word goes far beyond this. Ultimately to be anathematized by the Church of Rome means to be cut off from the Church which is the source of salvation. Consequently, the term indirectly involves a condemnation of the individual anathematized to hell unless there is repentance and a return to the Roman Church and an embracing of its teachings.

Thus, it is important to understand that, according to the Church of Rome, apart from an embracing of its doctrines there is no salvation. This is clearly seen from the teaching of Vatican I on the meaning of saving faith and the role of the Church in defining the doctrinal content of such faith. Therefore, the gospel according to Rome consists of justification that is a process and is dependent upon the works and merits of the individual, the Roman Catholic sacraments as a means of salvation, the full embracing of the Roman Catholic teaching of papal infallibilty and jurisdiction and the Marian doctrines of the immaculate conception and assumption. Unless one believes these things and submits to them there is no justification or salvation. Is this the biblical gospel delineated in the scriptures and proclaimed by the apostles? Most assuredly not! It is a fundamental denial of the biblical teaching of salvation. As such there is no grounds for the appeal for unity of those involved in the ECT accord, for the Evangelical and Roman Catholic Churches are not unified on the meaning of the gospel. Unity that is not grounded in truth is a false political uniformity that must be vigorously yet graciously opposed by all who love the scriptures and who would stand true to the gospel of the Lord Jesus Christ. Our ultimate loyalty must be to the person of Christ. The culture and the darkness that is enveloping it is not the overriding issue. The ultimate issue is truth and on that basis the evangelical and Roman Catholic Churches are irreparably divided.

VATICAN I

Vatican I states that it is necessary for salvation that men and women not only believe all that is revealed in scripture but also everything which is defined and proposed by the Church as having been divinely revealed. To reject anything taught by the Roman Church is to reject saving faith and to forfeit justification and eternal life:

> Further, all those things are to be believed with divine and Catholic faith which are contained in the Word of God, written or handed down, and which the Church, either by a solemn judgment, or by her ordinary and universal magisterium, proposes for belief as having been divinely revealed. And since, without faith, it is impossible to please God, and to attain to the *fellowship of his children, therefore*

without faith no one has ever attained justification, nor will any one obtain eternal life unless he shall have persevered in faith unto the end.[1]

Ludwig Ott explains the relationship of Dogmas defined by the Church and faith in these words:

By dogma in the strict sense is understood a truth immediately (formally) revealed by God which has been proposed by the Teaching Authority of the Church to be believed as such...All those things are to be believed by divine and Catholic faith which are contained in the Word of God written or handed down and which are proposed for our belief by the Church either in a solemn definition or in its ordinary and universal authoritative teaching. (Vatian I).

Two factors or elements may be distinguished in the concept of dogma:

A) An immediate Divine Revelation of the particular Dogma...i.e., the Dogma must be immediately revealed by God either explicitly (explicite) or inclusively (implicite), and therefore be contained in the sources of Revelation (Holy Writ or Tradition)

B) The Promulgation of the Dogma by the Teaching Authority of the Church (propositio Ecclesiae). *This implies, not merely the promulgation of the Truth, but also the obligation on the part of the Faithful of believing the Truth.* This promulgation by the Church may be either in an extraordinary manner through a solemn decision of faith made by the Pope or a General Council (Iudicium solemns) or through the ordinary and general teaching power of the Church (Magisterium ordinarium et universale). The latter may be found easily in the catechisms issued by the Bishops.

Dogma in its strict signification is the object of both Divine Faith (Fides Divina) and Catholic Faith (Fides Catholica); it is the object of the Divine Faith...by reason of its Divine Revelation; it is the object of Catholic Faith...on account of its infallible doctrinal definition by the Church. *If a baptised person deliberately denies or doubts a dogma properly so-called, he is guilty of the sin of heresy (Codex Iuris Canonici 1325, Par. 2), and automatically becomes subject to the punishment of excommunication (Codex Iuris Canonici 2314, Par. I).*

As far as the content of justifying faith is concerned, the so-called fiducial faith does not suffice. What is demanded is theological or dogmatic faith (confessional faith) which consists in the firm acceptance of the Divine truths of Revelation, on the authority of God Revealing...*According to the testimony of Holy Writ, faith and indeed dogmatic faith, is the indispensable prerequisite for the achieving of eternal salvation* (emphasis added).[2]

This point is further emphasiszed by the Roman Catholic theologian John Hardon in his authoritative and popular catechism:

44. What must a Catholic believe with divine faith?

A Catholic must believe with divine faith the whole of revelation, which is contained in the written word of God and in Sacred Tradition.

45. Can a person be a Catholic if he believes most, but not all, the teachings of revelation?

A person cannot be a Catholic if he rejects even a single teaching that he knows has been revealed by God.

46. What will happen to those who lack 'the faith necessary for salvation'?

Those will not be saved who lack the necessary faith because of their own sinful neglect or conduct. As Christ declared, 'He who does not believe will be condemned' (Mark 16:16).

47. Why is divine faith called catholic?

Divine faith is called catholic or universal because a believer must accept everything God has revealed. He may not be selective about what he chooses to believe.[3]

From the above citations it is clear that, according to Rome, it is incumbent upon all who would experience salvation that they embrace by faith the doctrinal content of the faith as it is authoritatively defined by Popes and Roman Catholic councils. Vatican I specifically states that one cannot experience justification and eternal life apart from a complete embracing of Dogmatic Faith which is the Faith as it is authoritatively defined by the Roman Catholic Church. Thus, as one analyzes the decrees, teachings and anathemas of the Popes made *ex cathedra* and those of the Councils such as Trent, Vatican I and Vatican II one can clearly ascertain the content of saving faith as it is defined by the Roman Catholic Church. In so doing it becomes very apparent that there is an inherent contradiction between the teaching of Vatican II and that of the popes and Councils which have preceeded it. Vatican II states that Protestants and Orthodox believers are 'separated brethren,' implying that they are in fact true Christians and can experience salvation outside of the Roman Catholic Church. This is a clear contradiction to the authoritative papal and conciliar teaching of the Roman Catholic Church prior to Vatican II. The popes in defining the Marian Dogmas have anathematized all who would in any way reject or doubt their teachings. And Trent and Vatican I state that they had met specifically to define dogmas of the faith in order to counter heresy, the teachings specifically held by Protestant and Orthodox believers, and both Councils condemn with anathema all who do not submit to their teachings and embrace with a positive faith what they have promulgated. As Trent states:

> With this view, in order to destroy the errors and to extirpate the heresies which have appeared in these our days on the subject of the said most holy sacraments, as well as those which have been revived from the heresies of old by our Fathers, as also those newly invented, and which are

exceedingly prejudicial to the purity of the Catholic Church and to the salvation of souls, the sacred and holy, ecumenical and general Synod of Trent, lawfully assembled in the Holy Ghost, the same legates of the Apostolic See presiding therein, adhering to the doctrine of the holy Scriptures, to the apostolic traditions, and to the consent of other councils and of the Fathers, has thought it fit that these present canons be established and decreed...[4]

And Vatican I states:

And this his salutary providence, which has been constantly displayed by other innumerable benefits, has been most manifestly proved by the abundant good results which Christendom has derived from ecummenical Councils, and particularly from that of Trent, although it was held in evil times. For, as a consequence, the sacred doctrines of the faith have been defined more closely, and set forth more fully, errors have been condemned and restrained...But while we recall with due thankfulness these and other signal benefits which the divine mercy has bestowed on the Church, especially by the last ecumenical Council, we can not restrain our bitter sorrow for the grave evils, which are principally due to the fact that the authority of that sacred Synod has been contemned, or its wise decrees neglected, by many. No one is ignorant of the heresies proscribed by the Fathers of Trent...Considering these things, how can the Church fail to be deeply stirred? For, even as God wills all men to be saved, and to arrive at the knowledge of the truth, even as Christ came to save what has perished, and to gather together the children of God who had been dispersed, so the Church, constituted by God the mother and teacher of nations, knows its own office as debtor to all, and is ever ready and watchful to raise the fallen, to support those who are falling, to embrace those who return, to confirm the good and to carry them on to better things. Hence, it can never forbear from witnessing to and proclaiming the truth of God. We, therefore, following the footsteps of our predecessors, have never ceased, as becomes our supreme Apostolic office, from teaching and defending Catholic truth, and condemning doctrines of error. And now, with the Bishops of the whole world assembled round us, and judging with us, congregated by our authority, and in the Holy Spirit, in this ecumenical Council, we, supported by the Word of God written and handed down as we received it from the Catholic Church, preserved with sacredness and set forth according to truth, have determined to profess and declare the salutary teaching of Christ from this Chair of Peter, and in the sight of all, proscribing and condemning, by the power given to us of God, all errors contrary thereto.[5]

According to Vatican I, all who reject its teachings are declared to be heretics and schismatics. This obviously applies in a direct sense to the Protestant and Orthodox Churches and its decrees are considered to be infallible by the Roman Catholic Church. Vatican I reaffirmed the Council of Trent and its decrees, and itself defined papal infallibility and primacy as doctrines necessary to be believed for salvation. And Vatican I was later reaffirmed by Vatican II:

In order that the episcopate itself might be one and undivided, He placed Peter over the other apostles, and instituted in him a permanent and visible source and foundation of unity of faith and fellowship (Cf. *Vatican Council I, Session 4, the dogmatic constitution 'Pastor aeternus')*. And all this teaching about the institution, the perpetuity, the force and reason for the sacred primacy of the Roman Pontiff and of his infallible teaching authority, this sacred Synod again proposes to be firmly believed by all the faithful.[6]

Thus, if we ask, what is the content of the Faith defined by the Roman Catholic Church, which all men must embrace to experience salvation, what would the overall doctrines consist of? The Church affirms first of all the 'Rule of Faith' as defined by the Apostles Creed. This was stated in the opening sessions of the Council of Trent. But in addition to this common body of Doctrine shared by the Roman Catholic, Protestant and Orthodox Churches there have been other doctrines introduced into the deposit of Faith by the Roman Catholic Church. It is these that we are mainly concerned with which have been promulgated by several popes and the Councils of Trent and Vatican I.

These dogmas can be summarized in the statements that follow. These are not an exhaustive listing but a fair summarization of the teachings defined by the Roman Church by specific popes and these two councils. To deny any of these teachings and to refuse to embrace them with a positive faith is to come under an anathema and to experience loss of saving faith:

• An individual must believe that the popes are infallible when teaching *ex cathedra.*

• One must believe that the Bishops of Rome have been given authority by Christ to rule the Church universal.

• One must be submitted to the Bishop of Rome in all areas of faith, morals, discipline and government of the Church.

• The Roman Catholic Church alone has the right to interpret Scripture and its interpretations are infallible.

• One must accept the Apocrypha as Scripture and as part of the Canon.

• There is no salvation outside of the Roman Catholic Church.

• One must believe that the Roman Catholic sacraments are necessary for salvation and that there specific number is seven.

• An individual must repudiate the teaching that the imputed righteousness of Christ is the basis for justification.

• One must embrace the teaching that justification is not by faith alone but by human works cooperating with grace and by participation in the sacraments.

• One must believe that human works cooperating with grace merit eternal life.

• One must accept the teaching that water baptism is necessary for salvation as it is the instrumental means of regeneration even for infants.

• One must believe that the Mass is a propitiatory sacrifice for sin.

• One must believe that in the eucharist the bread and wine is transformed into the literal body and blood of Christ at the words of consecration (Transubstantiation).

• It is necessary to believe that confession of sins to a Roman Catholic priest and receiving his absolution and performing acts of penance is the only way to receive forgiveness of sins after baptism.

• One must embrace the teachings of the immaculate conception and Assumption of Mary.

• One must accept the Roman Catholic teaching on Purgatory.

⌐ 3 ⌐

THE PAPACY

Primacy and Jurisdiction

The Bull *Unam Sanctam* by Pope Boniface VIII
(1302 A.D.)

Boniface, Bishop, Servant of the servants of God. For perpetual remembrance:

Urged on by our faith, we are obliged to believe and hold that there is one holy, catholic, and apostolic Church. And we firmly believe and profess that outside of her there is no salvation nor remission of sins, as the bridegroom declares in the Canticles, 'My dove, my undefiled, is but one; she is the only one of her mother; she is the choice one of her that bare her.' And this represents the one mystical body of Christ, and of this body Christ is the head, and God is the head of Christ. In it there is one Lord, one faith, one baptism. For in the time of the Flood there was the single ark of Noah, which prefigures the one Church, and it was finished according to the measure of one cubit and had one Noah for pilot and captain, and outside of it every living creature on the earth, as we read, was destroyed. And this Church we revere as the only one, even as the Lord saith by the prophet, 'Deliver my soul from the sword, my darling from the power of the dog.' He prayed for his soul, that is, for himself, head and body. And this body he called one

23

body, that is, the Church, because of the single bridegroom, the unity of the faith, the sacraments, and the love of the Church. She is that seamless shirt of the Lord which was not rent but was allotted by the casting of lots. Therefore, this one and single Church has one head and not two heads—for had she two heads, she would be a monster—that is, Christ and Christ's vicar, Peter and Peter's successor. For the Lord said unto Peter, 'Feed my sheep.' 'My,' he said, speaking generally and not particularly, 'these and those,' by which it is to be understood that all the sheep are committed unto him. *So, when the Greeks and others say that they were not committed to the care of Peter and his successors, they must confess that they are not of Christ's sheep, even as the Lord says in John, 'There is one fold and one shepherd'* (emphasis added).

That in her and within her power are two swords, we are taught in the Gospels, namely, the spiritual sword and the temporal sword. For when the Apostles said, 'Lo, here'—that is, in the Church—are two swords, the Lord did not reply to the Apostles 'it is too much,' but 'it is enough.' It is certain that whoever denies that the temporal sword is in the power of Peter hearkens ill to the words of the Lord which he spake, 'Put up thy sword into its sheath.' Therefore, both are in the power of the Church, namely, the spirtual sword and the temporal sword; the latter is to be used for the Church, the former by the Church; the former by the hand of the priest, the latter by the hand of princes and kings, but at the nod and sufferance of the priest. The one sword must of necessity be subject to the other, and the temporal authority to the spiritual. For the Apostle said, 'There is no power but of God, and the powers that be are ordained of God'; and they would not have been ordianed unless one sword had been made subject to the other, and even as the lower is subjected to the other for higher things. For, according to Dionysius, it is a divine law that the lowest things are made by mediocre things to attain to the highest. For it is not according to the law of the universe that all things in an equal way and immediately should reach their end, but the lowest through the mediocre and the lower through their higher. But that the spiritual power excells the earthly power in dignity and worth, we will the more clearly acknowledge just in proportion as the spiritual is higher than the temporal. And this we perceive quite distinctly from the donation of the tithe and functions of benediction and sanctification, from the mode in which the power was received, and the government of the subjected realms. For truth being the witness, the spiritual power has the functions of establishing the temporal power and sitting in judgment on it if it should prove not to be good. And to the Church and the Church's power the prophecy of Jeremiah attests: 'See, I have set thee this day over the nations and kingdoms to pluck up and to break down and to destroy and to overthrow, to build and to plant.'

And if the earthly power deviate from the right path, it is judged by the spiritual power; but if a minor spiritual power deviate from the right path, the lower in rank is judged by its superior; but if the supreme power [the papacy] deviate, it can be judged not by man, but by God alone. And so the Apostle testifies, 'He that is spiritual judges all things, but he himself is judged by no man.' But this authority, although it be given to a man, and though it be exercised by a man, is not a human but a divine power given by divine word of mouth to Peter and confirmed to Peter and to his successors by Christ himself, whom Peter confessed, even him whom Christ called the Rock. For the Lord said to Peter himself, 'Whatsoever thou shalt bind on earth,' etc. Whoever, therefore, resists this power so ordained by God, resists the ordinance of God, unless perchance he imagines two principles to exist, as did Manichaeus, which we pronounce false and heretical. For Moses testified that God created heaven and earth not in the beginnings but 'in the beginning.'

Furthermore, that every human creature is subject to the Roman pontiff,—this we declare, say, define, and pronounce to be altogether necessary to salvation.[7]

THE NEW CATHOLIC ENCYCLOPEDIA

The New Catholic Encyclopedia gives the following historical background to the papal decree *Uñam Sanctam:*

> A bull of Boniface VIII, issued Nov. 18, 1302, in which the unity of the Church and the spiritual authority are proclaimed. Occasioned by the second major struggle between Boniface VIII and Philip IV of France, *yet addressed to the universal Church*, the bull declares that there is one, holy, catholic, and apostolic church outside of which there is neither salvation nor remission of sins. The Church represents the Mystical Body, whose head is Christ and in which there is one Lord, one faith, and one Baptism. Therefore, this one body, unlike a monster, has only one head, Christ and His vicar, Peter and his successors. Consequently, if anyone says that he has not been committed to Peter and his successors, he necessarily declares that he is not of Christ's sheep...Finally, in its only dogmatic definition the bull concludes: 'We declare, state, and define that it is absolutely necessary for salvation that every human creature be subject to the Roman Pontiff.'[8]

VATICAN ONE

Chapter I: Of the Institution of the Apostolic Primacy in blessed Peter.

We therefore teach and declare that, according to the testimony of the Gospel, the primacy of jurisdiction over the universal Church of God was immediately and directly promised and given to blessed Peter the Apostle by Christ the Lord. For it was to Simon alone, to whom he had already said: 'Thou shalt be called Cephas,' that the Lord after the confession made by him, saying: 'Thou art the Christ, the Son of the living God,' addressed these solemn words: 'Blessed art thou, Simon Bar-Jona, because flesh and blood have not revealed it to thee, but my Father who is in heaven. And I say to thee that thou art Peter; and upon this rock I will build my Church, and the gates of hell shall not prevail against it. And I will give to thee the keys of the kingdom of heaven. And whatsoever thou shalt bind on earth, it shall be bound also in heaven; and whatsoever thou shalt loose on earth, it shall be loosed also in heaven.' And it was upon Simon alone that Jesus after his resurrection bestowed the jurisdiction of chief pastor and ruler over all his fold in the words: 'Feed my lambs; feed my sheep.' At open variance with this clear doctrine of Holy Scripture as it has been ever understood by the Catholic Church are the perverse opinions of those who, while they distort the form of government established by Christ the Lord in his Church, deny that Peter in his single person, preferably to all the other Apostles, whether taken separately or together, was endowed by Christ with a true and proper primacy of jurisdiction; or of those who assert that the same primacy was not bestowed immediately and directly upon blessed Peter himself, but upon the Church, and through the Church on Peter as her minister.

If any one, therefore, shall say that blessed Peter the Apostle was not appointed the Prince of all the Apostles and the visible Head of the whole Church militant; or that the same directly and immediately received from the same our Lord Jesus Christ a primacy of honor only, and not of true and proper jurisdiction: let him be anathema.

Chapter II: On the Perpetuity of the Primacy of blessed Peter in the Roman Pontiffs.

That which the Prince of Shepherds and great Shepherd of the sheep, Jesus Christ our Lord, established in the person of the blessed Apostle Peter to secure the perpetual welfare and lasting good of the Church, must, by the same institution, necessarily remain unceasingly in the Church; which, being founded upon the Rock, will stand firm to the end of the world. For none can doubt, and it is known to all ages, that the holy and blessed Peter, the Prince and Chief of the Apostles, the pillar of the faith and foundation of the Catholic Church, received the keys of the kingdom from our Lord Jesus Christ, the Saviour and Redeèmer of mankind, and lives, presides, and judges, to this day and always, in his successors the Bishops of the Holy See of Rome, which was founded by him and consecrated by his blood. Whence, whosoever succeeds to Peter in this See, does by the institution of Christ himself obtain the Primacy of Peter over the whole Church. The disposiition made by Incarnate Truth therefore remains, and blessed Peter, abiding through the strength of the Rock in the power that he received, has not abandoned the direction of the Church. Wherefore it has at all times been necessary that every particular Church—that is to say, the faithful throughout the world—should agree with the Roman Church, on account of the greater authority of the princedom which this has received; that all being associated in the unity of that See whence the rights of communion spread to all, might grow together as members of one Head in the compact unity of the body.

If, then, any should deny that it is by institution of Christ the Lord, or by divine right, that blessed Peter should have a perpetual line of successors in the Primacy over the universal Church, or that the Roman Pontiff is the successor of blessed Peter in this primacy: let him be anathema.

Chapter III: On the Power and Nature of the Primacy of the Roman Pontiff.

Wherefore, resting on plain testimonies of the Sacred Writings, and adhering to the plain and express decrees both of our predecessors, the Roman Pontiffs, and of the General Councils, we renew the definition of the ecumenical Council of Florence, in virtue of which all the faithful of Christ must believe that the holy Apostolic See and the Roman Pontiff possesses the primacy over the whole world, and that the Roman Pontiff is the successor of blessed Peter, Prince of the

Apostles, and is true vicar of Christ, and head of the whole Church, and father and teacher of all Christians; and that full power was given to him in blessed Peter to rule, feed, and govern the universal Church by Jesus Christ our Lord; as is also contained in the acts of the General Councils and in the sacred Canons.

Hence we teach and declare that by the appointment of our Lord the Roman Church possesses a superiority of ordinary power over all other churches, and that this power of jurisdiction of the Roman Pontiff, which is truly episcopal, is immediate; to which all, of whatever right and dignity, both pastors and faithful, both individually and collectively, are bound, by their duty of hierarchial subordination and true obedience, to submit not only in matters which belong to faith and morals, but also in those which appertain to the discipline and government of the Church throughout the world, so that the Church of Christ may be one flock under one supreme pastor through the preservation of unity both of communion and of profession of the same faith with the Roman Pontiff. *This is the teaching of Catholic truth, from which no one can deviate without loss of faith and salvation.*

But so far is this power of the Supreme Pontiff from being any prejudice to the ordinary and immediate power of episcopal jurisdiction, by which Bishops, who have been set by the Holy Ghost to succeed and hold the place of the Apostles, feed and govern, each his own flock, as true pastors, that this their episcopal authority is really asserted, strengthened, and protected by the supreme and universal Pastor; in accordance with the words of St. Gregory the Great: 'My honor is the honor of the whole Church. My honor is the firm strength of my brethren. I am truly honored when the honor due to each and all is not withheld.

Further, from this supreme power possessed by the Roman Pontiff of governing the universal Church, it follows that he has the right of free communication with the pastors of the whole Church, and with their flocks, that these might be taught and ruled by him in the way of salvation. Wherefore we condemn and reject the opinions of those who hold that the communication between this supreme head and the pastors and their flocks can lawfully be impeded; or who make this communication subject to the will of the secular power, so as to maintain that whatever is done by the Apostolic See, or by its authority, for the government of the Church, can not have force or value unless it be confirmed by the assent of the secular power.

And since by the divine right of Apostolic primacy the Roman Pontiff is placed over the universal Church, we further teach and declare that he is the supreme judge of the faithful, and that in all causes, the decision of which belongs to the Church, recourse may be had to his tribunal, and that none may re-open the judgment of the Apostolic See, than whose authority there is no greater, nor can any lawfully review its judgment. Wherefore they err from the right course who assert that it is lawful to appeal from the judgments of the Roman Pontiffs to an ecumenical Council, as to an authority higher than that of the Roman Pontiff.

If, then, any shall say that the Roman Pontiff has the office merely of inspection or direction, and not full and supreme power of jurisdiction over the universal Church, not only in things which belong to faith and morals, but also in those which relate to the discipline and government of the Church spread throughout the world; or assert that he possesses merely the principal part, and not all the fulness of this supreme power; or that that power which he enjoys is not ordinary and immediate, both over each and all the churches, and over each and all the pastors and the faithful: let him be anathema.[9]

CATECHISM OF THE CATHOLIC CHURCH

Simon Peter holds the first place in the college of the Twelve; Jesus entrusted a unique position to him. Through a revelation from the Father, Peter had confessed: 'You are the Christ, the Son of the living God.' Our Lord then declared to him: 'You are Peter, and on this rock I will build my Church, and the gates of Hades will not prevail against it.' Christ, 'the living stone,' thus assures his Church, built on Peter, of victory over the powers of death. Because of the faith he confessed Peter will remain the unshakeable ·rock of the Church. His mission will be to keep this faith from every lapse and to strengthen his brothers in it.

Jesus entrusted a specific authority to Peter: 'I will give you the keys of the kingdom of heaven, and whatever you bind on earth shall be bound in heaven, and whatever you loose on earth shall be loosed in heaven.' The 'power of the keys' designates authority to govern the house of God, which is the Church. Jesus, the Good Shepherd, confirmed this mandate after his Resurrection: 'Feed my sheep.' The power to 'bind and loose' connotes the authority to absolve sins, to pronounce doctrinal judgments, and to make disciplinary decisions in the Church. Jesus entrusted this authority to the Church through the ministry of the apostles and in particular through the ministry of Peter, the only one to whom he specifically entrusted the keys of the kingdom.

The words *bind and loose* mean: whomever you exclude from your communion, will be excluded from communion with God; whomever you receive anew into your communion, God will welcome back into his. ***Reconciliation with the Church is inseparable from reconciliation with God.***[10]

PAPAL INFALLIBILITY

VATICAN ONE

Moreover, that the supreme power of teaching is also included in the Apostolic primacy, which the Roman Pontiff, as the successor of Peter, Prince of the Apostles, possesses over the whole Church, this Holy See has always held, the perpetual practice of the Church confirms, and ecumenical councils also have declared, especially those in which the East with the West met in the union of faith and charity. For the Fathers of the Fourth Council of Constantinople, following in the footsteps of their predecessors, gave forth their solemn profession: *The first condition of salvation is to keep the rule of the true faith*. And because the sentence of our Lord Jesus Christ can not be passed by, who said: "Thou art Peter, and upon this rock I will build my Church,' these things which have been said are approved by events, because in the Apostolic See the Catholic religion and her holy and well-known doctrine has always been kept undefiled. Desiring, therefore, not to be in the least degree separated from the faith and doctrine of that See, we hope that we may deserve to be in the one communion, which the Apostolic See preaches, in which is the entire and true solidity of the Christian religion. And, with the approval of the Second Council of Lyons, the Greeks professed that the holy Roman Church enjoys supreme and full primacy and preeminence over the whole Catholic Church, which it truly and humbly acknowledges that it has received with the plentitude of power from our Lord himself in the person of the blessed Peter, Prince or Head of the Apostles, whose successor the Roman Pontiff is; and as the Apostolic See is bound before all others to defend the truth of faith, so also, if any questions regarding faith shall arise, they must be defined by its judgment. Finally, the Council of Florence defined: That the Roman Pontiff is the true vicar of Christ, and the head of the whole Church, and the father and teacher of all Christians; and that to him in blessed Peter was delivered by our Lord Jesus Christ the full power of feeding, ruling, and governing the whole Church.

To satisfy this pastoral duty, our predecessors ever made unwearied efforts that the salutary doctrine of Christ might be propogated among all the nations of the earth, and with equal care watched that it might be preserved genuine and pure where it had been received. Therefore the Bishops of the whole world, now singly, now assembled, following the long-established custom of churches, and the form of the ancient rule, sent word to this Apostolic See of those dangers especially which sprang up in matters of faith, that there the losses of faith might be most effectually repaired where the faith can not fail. And the Roman Pontiffs, according to the exegencies of times and circumstances, sometimes assembling ecumenical Councils, or asking for the mind of the Church scattered throughout the world, sometimes by particular Synods, sometimes using other helps which Divine Providence supplied, defined as to be held those things which with the help of God they had recognized as conformable with the sacred Scriptures and Apostolic traditions. For the Holy Spirit was not promised to the successors of Peter, that by his revelation they might make known new doctrine; but that by his assistance they might inviolably keep and faithfully expound the revelation or deposit of faith delivered through the Apostles. And, indeed, all the venerable Fathers have embraced, and the holy orthodox doctors have venerated and followed, their Apostolic doctrine; knowing most fully that this See of holy Peter remains ever free from all blemish of error according to the divine promise of the Lord our Saviour made to the Prince of his disciples: 'I have prayed for thee that thy faith fail not, and, when thou art converted, confirm thy brethren.'

This gift, then, of truth and never-failing faith was conferred by heaven upon Peter and his successors in his chair, that they might perform their high office for the salvation of all; that the whole flock of Christ, kept away by them from the poisonous food of error, might be nourished with the pasture of heavenly doctrine; that the occasion of schism being removed, the whole Church might be kept one, and, resting on its foundation, might stand firm against the gates of hell. But since in this very age, in which the salutary efficacy of the Apostolic office is most of all required, not a few are found who take away from its authority, we judge it altogether necessary solemnly to assert the prerogative which the only-begotten Son of God vouchsafed to join with the supreme pastoral office.

Therefore faithfully adhering to the tradition received from the beginning of the Christian faith, for the glory of God our Saviour, the exaltation of the Christian religion, and the salvation of Christian people, the sacred Council approving, we teach and define that it is a dogma divinely revealed: that the Roman Pontiff, when he speaks *ex cathedra*, that is, when in discharge of the office of pastor and doctor of all Christians, by virtue of his supreme Apostolic authority, he defines a doctrine regarding faith and morals to be held by the universal Church, by the divine assistance promised to him in blessed Peter, is possessed of that infallibility with which the divine redeemer willed that his Church should be endowed for defining doctrine regarding faith or morals; and that therefore such definitions of the Roman Pontiff are irreformable of themselves, and not from the consent of the Church. *But if any one—which may God avert—presume to contradict this our definition: let him be anathema.*[11]

VATICAN II

Bishops, teaching in communion with the Roman Pontiff, are to be respected by all as witnesses to divine and Catholic truth. In matters of faith and morals, the bishops speak in the name of Christ and the faithful are to accept their teaching and adhere to it with a religious assent of soul. This religious submission of will and mind must be shown in a special way to the authentic teaching authority of the Roman Pontiff, even when he is not speaking *ex cathedra*. That is, it must be shown in such a way that his supreme magesterium is acknowledged with reverence, the judgments made by him are sincerely adhered to, according to his manifest mind and will. His mind and will in the matter may be known chiefly either from the character of the documents, from his frequent repetition of the same doctrine, or from his manner of speaking.

Although the individual bishops do not enjoy the prerogative of infallibility, they can nevertheless proclaim Christ's doctrine infallibly...This infallibility with which the divine Redeemer willed His Church to be endowed in defining a doctrine of faith and morals extends as far as extends the deposit of divine revelation, which must be religiously guarded and faithfully expounded. This is the infallibility which the Roman Pontiff, the head of the college of bishops, enjoys in virtue of his office, when, as the supreme shepherd and teacher of all the faithful, who confirms his brethren in their faith (cf. Lk. 22:32), he proclaims by a definitive act some doctrine of faith or morals. Therefore his definitions, of themselves, are not from the consent of the Church, are justly styled irreformable, for they are pronounced with the assistance of the Holy Spirit, an assistance promised to him in blessed Peter. Therefore they need no approval of others, nor do they allow an appeal to any other judgment. For then the Roman Pontiff is not pronouncing judgment as a private person. Rather, as the supreme teacher of the universal Church, as one in whom the charism of the infallibility of the Church herself is individually present, he is expounding or defending a doctrine of Catholic faith.[12]

◻ 4 ◻

MARY

Since we have never ceased in humility and fasting to offer up our prayers and those of the Church to God the Father through his Son, that he might deign to direct and confirm our mind by the power of the Holy Ghost, after imploring the protection of the whole celestial court, and after invoking on our knees the Holy Ghost the Paraclete, under his inspiration we PRONOUNCE, DECLARE, AND DEFINE, unto the glory of the Holy and Indivisible Trinity, the honor and ornament of the holy Virgin the Mother of God, for the exaltation of the Catholic faith and increase of the Christian religion, by the authority of our Lord Jesus Christ and the blessed Apostles Peter and Paul, and in our own authority, that the doctrine which holds the blessed Virgin Mary to have been, from the first instant of her conception, by a singular grace and privilege of Almighty God, in view of the merits of Christ Jesus the Saviour of mankind, preserved free from all stain of original sin, was revealed by God, and is, therefore, to be firmly and constantly believed by all the faithful. *Therefore, if some should presume to think in their hearts otherwise than we have defined (which God forbid), they shall know and thoroughly understand that they are by their own judgment condemned, have*

37

made shipwreck concerning the faith, and fallen away from the
unity of the Church; and, moreover, that they, by this very act,
subject themselves to the penalties ordained by law, if, by word or
writing, or any other external means, they dare to signify what they
think in their hearts.[13]

Vatican II on the Immaculate Conception of Mary

It is no wonder, then, that the usage prevailed among the holy
Fathers whereby they called the Mother of God entirely holy
and free from all stain of sin, fashioned by the Holy Spirit into
a kind of new substance and new creature. Adorned from the
first instance of her conception with the splendors of an
entirely unique holiness, the Virgin of Nazareth is, on God's
command, greeted by an angel messenger as 'full of grace' (cf.
Lk. 1:28)...Embracing God's saving will with a full hreart and
impeded by no sin, she devoted herself totally as a handmaid
of the Lord to the person and work of her Son...Finally,
preserved free from all guilt of original sin, the Immaculate
Virgin was taken up body and soul into heavenly glory upon
the completion of her earthly sojourn.[14]

THE DECREE OF POPE PIUS XII ON THE ASSUMPTION OF MARY FROM THE BULL *MUNIFICENTISSIMUS DEUS* (A.D. 1950).

All these proofs and considerations of the holy Fathers and the
theologians are based upon the Sacred Writings as their
ultimate foundation. These set the loving Mother of God as it
were before our very eyes as most intimately joined to her
divine Son and as always sharing His lot. Consequently it
seems impossible to think of her, the one who conceived
Christ, brought Him forth, nursed Him with her milk, held
Him in her arms, and clasped Him to her breast, as being apart
from Him in body, even though not in soul, after this earthly
life. Since our Redeemer is the Son of Mary, He could not do
otherwise, as the perfect observer of God's law, than to honor,
not only His eternal Father, but also His most beloved

Mother. And, since it was within His power to grant her this great honor, to preserve her from the corruption of the tomb, we must believe that He really acted this way.

Hence the revered Mother of God, from all eternity joined in a hidden way with Jesus Christ in one and the same decree of predestination, immaculate in her conception, a most perfect virgin in her divine motherhood, the noble associate of the divine Redeemer who has won a complete triumph over sin and its consequences, finally obtained, as the supreme culmination of her privileges, that she should be preserved free from the corruption of the tomb and that like her Son, having overcome death, she might be taken up body and soul to the glory of heaven where, as Queen, she sits in splendor at the right hand of her Son, the immortal King of the Ages.

For which reason, after we have poured forth prayers of supplication again and again to God, and have invoked the light of the Spirit of Truth, for the glory of Almighty God Who has lavished His special affection upon the Virgin Mary, for the honor of her Son, the immortal King of the Ages and the Victor over sin and death, for the increase of the glory of that same august Mother, and for the joy and exultation of the entire Church; by the authority of our Lord Jesus Christ, of the blessed Apostles Peter and Paul, and by Our own authority, *We pronounce, declare, and define it to be a divinely revealed dogma: that the Immaculate Mother of God, the ever Virgin Mary, having completed the course of her earthly life, was assumed body and soul into heavenly glory.*

Hence, if anyone, which God forbid, should dare wilfully to deny or call into doubt that which we have defined, let him know that he has fallen away completely from the divine and Catholic faith...It is forbidden to any man to change this, Our declaration, pronouncement, and definition or, by rash attempt, to oppose and counter it. If any man should presume to make such an attempt, let him know that he will incur the wrath of Almighty God and of the Blessed Apostles Peter and Paul.[15]

VATICAN II ON THE ASSUMPTION OF MARY

Finally, preserved free from all guilt of original sin, the Immaculate Virgin was taken up body and soul into heavenly glory upon the completion of her earthly sojourn...For, taken up into heaven, she did not lay aside this saving role, but by her manifold acts of intercession continues to win for us gifts of eternal salvation...Therefore the Blessed Virgin is invoked by the Church under the titles of Advocate, Auxiliatrix, Adjutrix, and Mediatrix...As the most holy Mother of God she was, after her Son, exalted by divine grace above all angels and men. Hence the Church appopriately honors her with special reverence...In all perils and needs, the faithful have fled prayerfully to her protection.[16]

▬ 5 ▬

JUSTIFICATION

The Roman Catholic Church teaches that justification is a cooperative work between God and man. It explicitly condemns the truth of the imputed righteousness of Christ himself as the basis for justification. But scripture teaches that man is justified by the righteousness of God (Rom. 3-5; 10:1-4; Phil 3:8-10). This righteousness is specifically described as being the righteousness of Christ himself in his perfect life and work of atonement (Rom. 5:9, 16-19). It further teaches that just as man's sin was imputed to Christ so his righteousness (the righteousness of God) is imputed as a gift to those who come to Christ in faith (Rom. 4:1-6) which secures an eternal justification for that individual. Scripture teaches therefore that justification is not based upon any works of man but solely upon the work and merit of Christ (Rom. 3:28; 4:1-6; Eph. 2:8-9; Gal. 2:16; Tit. 3:5-6). The Church of Rome, however, teaches that justification is the result of grace infused in the soul of man which enables an individual to do works of righteousness which then become the basis of one's justification. The biblical phrase, the righteousness of God, is interpreted by Rome to mean, not the righteousness of Christ himself, but what the *Catechism of the Catholic Church* calls the rectitude of Divine love (Paragraph 1992). The righteousness of God is love infused into the soul of man with faith by which a man lives a life pleasing to God which then justifies him before God. In Roman Catholic theology, what Christ merited on the cross was not a full and complete

41

salvation but grace which is given as a gift by which a person cooperates with God to achieve and merit justification by personal works. Justification is not a declaration of righteousness based upon the imputed righteousness of Jesus Christ but a declaration of the *believer's* righteousness before the judgment seat of God based on an infusion of grace in a believer's life. This means that justification is not grounded exclusively in the work of Christ but also in the works and merits of the individual. The Reformation and biblical teaching of grace *alone*, by Christ *alone*, by faith *alone* is explicitly condemned by the Church of Rome and it states that apart from the repudiation of the Reformation gospel and adherence to its teachings on justification and salvation that one does not possess saving faith or justification. These thoughts are clearly expressed by Roman Catholic theologian Ludwig Ott and the Council of Trent in the following statements:

LUDWIG OTT

According to the teaching of the Council of Trent, sanctifying grace is the sole formal cause of justification...This means that the infusion of sanctifying grace effects the eradication of sin as well as inner sanctification. With this the Council rejects the doctrine of double justice which was expounded by some Reformers (Calvin, Martin Butzer), and also by individual Catholic theologians (Girolamo Seripando, Gasparo Contrarini, Albert Pighius, Johannes Gropper), which taught that the forgiveness of sins was accomplished by the imputed justice of Christ, positive sanctification, however, by a righteousness inhering in the soul.

According to the teaching of the Council of Trent, faith is 'the beginning of human salvation, the basis and the root of all justice...As far as the content of justifying faith is concerned, the so–called fiducial faith does not suffice. What is demanded is theological or dogmatic faith...which consists in the firm acceptance of the Divine truths of Revelation, on the authority of God Revealing...According to the testimony of Holy Writ, faith and indeed dogmatic faith, is the indispensable prerequisite for the achieving of eternal salvation.

When St. Paul teaches that we are saved by faith without the works of the Law (Rom. 3:28)...he understands by faith, living faith, active through love (Gal. 5:6); by works of the law he means the works of the law of the Old Testament, for example, circumcision; by justification, the inner purification and sanctification of the non-Christian sinner by the acceptance of the Christian Faith. When *St. James*, in apparent contradiction to this, teaches that we are justified by works, not merely by faith (James 2:24)...he **understands** by faith, dead faith (James 2:17; Mt. 7:21); by works, the good works proceeding from Christian Faith; *by justification, the declaration of the righteousness of the Christian before the judgment seat of God.*

The Council of Trent teaches that *for the justified eternal life is both a gift or grace promised by God and a reward for his works and merits.*[17]

THE COUNCIL OF TRENT

Chapter IV: By which words a description of the Justification of the impious is indicated—as being a translation, from that state wherein man is born a child of Adam, to the state of grace, and of the adoption of the sons of God, through the second Adam, Jesus Christ, our Saviour. And this translation, since the promulgation of the the Gospel, can not be effected, without the laver of regeneration, or the desire thereof, as it is written: unless a man be born again of water and the Holy Ghost, he can not enter into the Kingdom of God.

Chapter V: The Synod furthermore declares, that, in adults, the beginning of the said Justification is to be derived from the prevenient grace of God, through Jesus Christ, that is to say, from his vocation, whereby, without any merits existing on their parts, they are called; that so they, who by sins were alienated from God, may be disposed through his quickening and assisting grace, to convert themselves to their own justification, by freely assenting to and co-operating with that said grace: in such sort' that, while God touches the heart of man by the illumination of the Holy Ghost, neither is man himself utterly inactive while he receives that inspiration, forasmuch as he is also able to reject it; yet is he not able, by his own free will, without the grace of God, to move himself unto justice in his sight.

Chapter VI: Now they (adults) are disposed unto the said justice, when, excited and assisted by divine grace, conceiving faith by hearing, they are freely moved towards God, believing those things to be true which God has revealed and promised—and this especially, that God justifies the impious by his grace, through the redemption that is in Christ Jesus; and when, understanding themselves to be sinners, they, by turning themselves, from the fear of divine justice whereby they are profitably agitated, to consider the mercy of God, are raised unto hope, confiding that God will be propitious to them for Christ's sake; and they begin to love him as the fountain of all justice; and are therefore moved against sins by a certain hatred and detestation, to wit, by that penitence which must be performed before baptism: lastly, when they purpose to receive baptism, to begin a new life, and to keep the commandments of God. Concerning this disposition it is written: He that cometh to God, must believe that he is, and is a rewarder to them that seek him; and, Be of good faith, son, thy sins are forgiven thee; and, The fear of the Lord driveth out sin; and, Do penance, and be baptized every one of you in the name of Jesus Christ, for the remission of your sins, and you shall receive the gift of the Holy Ghost; and, Going, therefore, teach ye all nations, baptizing them in the name of the Father, and of the Son, and of the Holy Ghost; finally, Prepare your hearts unto the Lord.

Chapter VII: *This disposition, or preparation, is followed by*

Justification itself, which is not the remission of sins merely, but also the sanctification and renewal of the inward man, through the voluntary reception of the grace, and of the gifts, whereby man of unjust becomes just, and of an enemy a friend, so that he may be an heir according to the hope of life everlasting. Of this Justification the causes are these: the final cause indeed is the glory of God and of Jesus Christ, and life everlasting; while the efficient cause is a merciful God who washes and sanctifies gratuitously, signing, and anointing with the holy Spirit of promise, who is the pledge of our inheritance; but the meritorious cause is his most beloved only-begotten, our Lord Jesus Christ, who, when we were enemies, for the exceeding charity wherewith he loved us, merited Justification for us by his most holy Passion on the wood of the cross, and made satisfaction for us unto God the Father; the instrumental cause is the sacrament of baptism, which is the sacrament of faith, without which (faith) no man was ever justified; lastly, the alone formal cause is the justice of God, not that whereby he himself is just, but that whereby he maketh us just, that, to wit, with which we, being endowed by him, are renewed in the spirit of our mind, and we are not only reputed, but are truly called, and are just, receiving justice within us, each one according to his own measure, which the Holy Ghost distributes to everyone as he wills, and according to each one's proper disposition and co-operation. For, although no one can be just, but he to whom the merits of the Passion of our Lord Jesus Christ are communicated, yet is this done in the said justification of the impious, when by the merit of that same most holy Passion, the charity of God is poured forth by the Holy Spirit, in the hearts of those that are justified, and is inherent therein: whence, man, through Jesus Christ, in whom he is ingrafted, receives, in the said justification, together with the remission of sins, all these (gifts) infused at once, faith, hope, and charity.

For faith, unless hope and charity be added thereto, neither unites man perfectly with Christ, nor makes him a living member of his body. For which reason it is most truly said, that faith without works is dead and profitless; and, In Christ Jesus neither circumcision availeth any thing nor uncircumcision, but faith which worketh by charity. This faith, Catechumens beg of the Church—agreeably to a tradition of the apostles—previously to the sacrament of Baptism; when they beg for the faith which bestows life everlasting, which, without hope and charity, faith can not bestow: whence also do they immediately hear that word of Christ: If thou wilt enter into life, keep the commandments. Wherefore, when receiving true and Christian justice, they are bidden, immediately on being born again, to preserve it pure and spotless, as the first robe given them through Jesus Christ in lieu of that which Adam, by his disobedience, lost for himself and for us, that so they may bear it before the judgment-seat of our Lord Jesus Christ, and may have life eternal.

Chapter X: Having, therefore, been thus justified, and made the friends and domestics of God, advancing from virtue to virtue, they are renewed, as the apostle says, day by day; that is, by mortifying the members of their own flesh, and by presenting them as instruments of justice unto sanctification, they, through the observance of the commandments of God and of the Church, faith co-operating with good works, increase in that justice which they have received through the grace of Christ, and are still further justified, as it is written: He that is just, let him be justified still; and again, Be not afraid to be justified even to death; and also, Do you see that by works a man is justified, and not by faith only. And this increase of justification holy Church begs, when she prays, 'Give unto us, O Lord, increase of faith, hope, and charity.

Chapter XIV: *As regards those who, by sin, have fallen from the received grace of Justification, they may be again justified, when, God exciting them, through the sacrament of Penance they shall have attained to the recovery, by the merit of Christ, of the grace lost*: for this manner of Justification is of the fallen the reparation: which the holy Fathers have aptly called a second plank after the shipwreck of grace lost. *For, on behalf of those who fall into sins after baptism, Christ Jesus instituted the sacrament of Penance*, when he said, Receive ye the Holy Ghost, whose sins you shall forgivè, they are forgiven them, and whose sins you shall retain, they are retained. Whence it is to be taught, that *the penitence of a Christian, after his fall, is very different from that at (his) baptism; and that therein are included not obnly a cessation from sins, and a detestation thereof, or, a contrite and humble heart, but also the sacramental confession of the said sins, - at least in desire, and to made in its season, - and sacerdotal absolution; and likewise satisfaction by fasts, alms, prayers, and the other pious exercises of the spiritual life; not indeed for the eternal punishment—which is, together with the guilt, remitted, either by the sacrament, or by desire of the sacrament—but for the temporal punishment*, which, as the sacred writings teach, is not always wholly remitted, as is done in baptism, to those who, ungrateful to the grace of God which they have received, have grieved the Holy Spirit, and have not feared to violate the temple of God. Concerning which penitence is written: Be mindful whence thou art fallen; do penance, and do the first works. And again: The sorrow that is according to God worketh penancè steadfast unto salvation. And again: Do penance, and bring forth fruits worthy of penance.

Chapter XV: In opposition also to the subtle wits of certain men, who, by pleasing speeches and good words, seduce the hearts of the innocent, it is to be maintained, that the received grace of Justification is lost, not only by infidelity whereby even faith itself is lost, but also by any other mortal sin whatever, though faith be not lost; thus defending the doctrine of the divine law, which excludes from the kingdom of God not only the unbelieving, but the faithful also (who are) fornicators, adulterers, effeminate, liers with mankind, thieves, covetous, drunkards, railers, extortioners, and all others who commit deadly sins; from which, with the help of divine grace, they can refrain, and on account of which they are separated from the grace of Christ.

Chapter XVI: And, for this cause, *life eternal is to be proposed to those working well unto the end, and hoping in God through Jesus Christ, and as a reward which is according to the promise of God himself, to be faithfully rendered to their good works and merits.* For this is that crown of justice which the apostle declared was, after his fight and course, laid up for him, to be rendered to him by the just Judge, and not only to him, but alas to all that love his coming. For, whereas Jesus Christ himself continually infuses his virtue into the said justified—as the head into the members, and the vine into the branches—and this virtue always precedes and accompanies and follows their good works, which without it could not in any wise be pleasing and meritorious before God—we must believe that nothing further is wanting to the justified, to prevent their being accounted to have, by those very works which have been done in God, fully satisfied the divine law according to the state of this life, and to have truly merited eternal life, to be obtained also in its (due) time, if so be, however, that they depart in grace: seeing that Christ, our Saviour, saith: If any one shall drink of the water that I will give him, he ˙shall not thirst forever; but it shall become in him a fountain of water springing up unto life everlasting.

After this Catholic doctrine on justification, which whosoever does not faithfully and firmly accept cannot be justified, it seemed good to the holy council to add these canons, that all may know not only what they must hold and follow, but what to avoid and shun:

Canon I: If any one saith, that man may be justified before God by his own works, whether done through the teaching of human nature, or that of the law, without the grace of God through Jesus Christ: let him be anathema.

Canon III: If any one saith, that without the prevenient inspirtaion of the Holy Ghost, and without his help, man can believe, hope, love, or be penitent as he ought, so that the grace of Justification may be bestowed upon him: let him be anathema.

Canon VII. If any one saith, that all works done before Justification, in whatsoever way they be done, are truly sins, or merit the hatred of God; that the more earnestly one strives to dispose himself for grace, the more greviously he sins, let him be anathema.

Canon IX. *If any one saith that by faith alone the impious is justified, in such wise as to mean, that nothing else is required to cooperate in order to obtaining the grace of Justification*, and that it is not in any way necessary that he be prepared and disposed by the movement of his own will, *let him be anathema*.

Canon X. If any one saith, that men are just without the *justice of Christ*, whereby he merited for us to be justified; *or that it is by that justice itself that they are formally just: let him be anathema*.

Canon XI. If any one saith, that men are justified, either by the sole imputation of the justice of Christ, or by the sole remission of sins, to the exclusion of the grace and the charity which is poured forth in their hearts by the Holy Ghost, and is inherent in them; or even that the grace, whereby we are justified is only the favor of God: let him be anathema.

Canon XXIV. *If any one saith, that the justice received is not preserved and also increased before God through good works; but that the said works are merely the fruits and signs of Justification obtained, but not a cause of the increase thereof: let him be anathema*.

Canon XXVI. If anyone saith that the just ought not for the good works done in God, to expect and hope for an eternal reward from God through His mercy and the merit of Jesus

Christ, if by doing well and keeping the commandments they persevere to the end, let him be anathema.

Canon XXIX. *If any one saith, that he who has fallen after baptism is not able by the grace of God to rise again; or, that he is able indeed to recover the justice which he has lost, but by faith alone without the sacrament of Penance, contrary to what the holy Roman and universal Church—instructed by Christ and his Apostles—has hitherto professed, observed, and taught: let him be anathema.*

Canon XXX. If any one saith, that, after the grace of Justification has been received, to every penitent sinner the guilt is remitted, and the debt of eternal punishment is blotted out in such wise that there remains not any debt of temporal punishment to be discharged either in this world, or in the next in Purgatory, before the entrance into the kingdom of heaven can be opened (to him): let him be anathema

Canon XXXI. If anyone says that the one justified sins when he performs good works with a view to an eternal reward, let him be anathema.

Canon XXXII. *If any one saith, that the good works of one that is justified are in such manner the gifts of God, that they are not also the good merits of him that is justified, by the good works which he performs through the grace of God and the merit of Jesus Christ, whose living member he is, does not truly merit increase of grace, eternal life, and the attainment of that eternal life—if so be, however, that he depart in grace,—and also an increase of glory: let him be anathema..*[18]

THE COUNCIL OF TRENT

The Sacraments And Justification:

For the completion of the salutary doctrine on Justification...it

hath seemed suitable to treat of the most holy Sacraments of the Church, through which all true justice either begins, or being begun is increased, or being lost is repaired. With this view, in order to destroy the errors and to extirpate the heresies which have appeared in these our days on the subject of the said most holy sacraments, as well as those which have been revived from the heresies of old by our Fathers, as also those newly invented, and which are exceedingly prejudicial to the purity of the Catholic Church and to the salvation of souls, the sacred and holy, ecumenical and general Synod of Trent, lawfully assembled in the Holy Ghost, the same legates of the Apostolic See presiding therein, adhering to the doctrine of the holy Scriptures, to the apostolic traditions, and to the consent of other councils and of the Fathers, has thought it fit that these present canons be established and decreed...

Canon I. If any one saith, that the sacraments of the New Law were not all instituted by Jesus Christ, our Lord; or, that there are more, or less, than seven, to wit, Baptism, Confirmation, the Eucharist, Penance, Extreme Unction, Order and Matrimony; or even that any of these seven is not truly and properly a sacrament, let him be anathema.

Canon IV. *If any one saith, that the sacraments of the New Law are not necessary unto salvation,* but superfluous; *and that, without them, or without the desire thereof, men obtain from God, through faith alone, the grace of justification,* though all [the sacraments] are not indeed necessary for each individual, *let him be anathema.*

Canon VI. If any one saith, that the sacraments of the New Law do not contain the grace which they signify; or, that they do not confer that grace on those who do not place an obstacles thereunto; as though they were merely outward signs of grace or justice received through faith, and certain marks of the Christian profession, whereby believers are distinguished amongst men from unbelievers, let him be anathema.[19]

CATECHISM OF THE CATHOLIC CHURCH

The first work of the grace of the Holy Spirit is *conversion*, effecting justification in accordance with Jesus' proclamation at the beginning of the Gospel: 'Repent for the kingdom of heaven is at hand.' Moved by grace, man turns toward God and away from sin, thus accepting forgiveness and righteousness from on high. 'Justification is not only the remission of sins, but also the sanctification and renewal of the interior man.'

Justification is at the same time the acceptance of God's righteousness through faith in Christ. Righteousness (or 'justice') here means the rectitude of divine love. With justification, faith, hope, and charity are poured into our hearts, and obedience to the divine will is granted us...Justification has been merited for us by the Passion of Christ who offered himself on the cross as a living victim, holy and pleasing to God, and whose blood has become the instrument of atonement for the sins of all men. Justification is conferred in Baptism, the sacrament of faith. It conforms us to the righteousness of God, who makes us inwardly just by the power of his mercy. [20]

- 6 -

The Meaning of Grace and Merit

Ludwig Ott

The God–Man Jesus Christ, by His vicarious atonement and His merit in the Redemption, achieved the reconciliation of humanity with God in principle and objectively. The Objective Redemption must be accepted by each man so that thereby he may bring to fruition in himself the subjective Redemption. The act of the application of the fruits of the Redemption to the individual man is called Justification...or Sanctification...The fruit of the Redemption is called grace...In the working-out of man's Subjective Redemption, God supports man, not merely by an inner principle, grace, but also by an outward principle, the efficacy of the Church in its doctrine, its guidance of men and its work of dispensing the grace of Christ through the Sacraments.

Habitual grace is a constant supernatural quality of the soul which sanctifies man intrinsically and makes him just and pleasing to God.

According to the teaching of the Council of Trent, 'no one can be just to whom the merits of Christ's Passion have not been communicated.'...It is a fundamental doctrine of St. Paul that salvation can be acquired only by the grace merited by Christ.

As God's grace is the presupposition and foundation of (supernatural) good works, by which man merits eternal life, so salutary works are, at the same time gifts of God and meritorious acts of man...By his good works the justified man really acquires a claim to supernatural reward from God...*A just man merits for himself through each good work* an increase in sanctifying grace, *eternal life* (if he dies in a state of grace) and an increase of heavenly glory.[21]

THE QUESTION AND ANSWER CATHOLIC CATECHISM

1074. What is habitual or sanctifying grace?

Habitual or sanctifying grace is a supernatural quality that dwells in the human soul, by which a person shares in the divine nature, becomes a temple of the Holy Spirit, a friend of God, his adopted child, an heir to the glory of heaven, and *able to perform actions meriting eternal life.*[22]

THE COUNCIL OF TRENT

Canon XXIV. *If any one saith, that the justice received is not preserved and also increased before God through good works; but that the said works are merely the fruits and signs of Justification obtained, but not a cause of the increase thereof: let him be anathema.*

Canon XXXII. *If any one saith, that the good works of one that is justified...does not truly merit increase of grace, eternal life, and the attainment of that eternal life— if so be, however, that he depart in grace,—and also an increase of glory: let him be anathema.*.[18]

Observation:

The above statements leave no room for doubt as to the oficial position of the Church of Rome on the issue of works and merit. Man's works are necessary as an addendum to the work of Christ for maintaining a state of justification before God and for meriting eternal life. Such teaching is clearly antithetical to the biblical meaning of grace and justification and is a distortion of the gospel of Jesus Christ. While the Roman Catholic Church teaches that in the initial expersince of justification at baptism there are no works of the individual involved (what is termed initial justification), this is not true in the ongoing experience of the person. This is because justification is not a finished work in Roman Catholic theology but an ongoing process equated with the works of sanctification. Therefore Rome teaches that works are necessary for salvation and are meritorius for the attaining of eternal life. In the Introduction, mention was made of the misrepresentation of Roman Catholic teaching in the ECT documents to make the Church of Rome appear virtually evangelical in its teaching. Those comments bear repeating here. In the ECT 2 document, the signers make the following statements regarding justification:

> Justification is central to the scriptural account of salvation, and its meaning has been much debated between Protestants and Catholics. We agree that justification is not earned by any good works or merits of our own; it is entirely God's gift, conferred through the Father's sheer graciousness, out of love that He bears us in His Son, who suffered on our behalf and rose from the dead for our justification. Jesus was 'put to death for our trespasses and raised for our justification' (Rom 4:25). In justification, God, on the basis of Christ's righteousness alone, declares us to be no longer his rebellious enemies but his forgiven friends, and by virtue of his declaration it is so.

Such a statement is a complete contradiction to the official teaching of Rome on justification. Rome would agree with this statement with respect to initial justification but certainly not for an understanding of its overall concept. Rome has officially condemned the statement as it stands in the ECT 2 document. But the signers of the document would lead us to believe that Roman Catholicism agrees withthis statement. It does not. Its position has been clearly defined in its councils and catechisms. To state that justification is based solely on the righteousness of Christ is a misrepresentation of the teaching of Rome. The Evangelical Church affirms this statement in the sense that it is Christ's righteousness alone *imputed* to the individual which justifies him eternally before God and which eliminates the necessity for any works whatsoever for the attaining of justification. The Church of Rome has officially condemned this teaching. While it teaches that Christ's righteousness alone merited the grace which is imparted to a believing sinner, it is not the righteousness of Christ himslef alone, imputed to the believer, that justifies but the works of the individual in cooperation with that grace. The signers of the ECT Documents are misleading people by carefully avoiding a full disclosure of what the Roman Catholic Church actaully means by the terms it uses.

⊐ 7 ⊐

BAPTISM

THE COUNCIL OF TRENT

On Justification: Chapter IV: By which words a description of the Justification of the impious is indicated—as being a translation, from that state wherein man is born a child of Adam, to the state of grace, and of the adoption of the sons of God, through the second Adam, Jesus Christ, our Saviour. And this translation, since the promulgation of the the Gospel, can not be effected, *without the laver of regeneration,* or the desire thereof, as it is written: unless a man be born again of water and the Holy Ghost, he can not enter into the Kingdom of God.

Canon II: If any one saith, that true and natural water is not of necessity for baptism, and, on that account, wrests, to some sort of metaphor, those words of our Lord Jesus Christ: Unless a man be born again of water and the Holy Ghost: let him be anathema.

Canon V: If any one saith, that baptism is free, that is, not necessary unto salvation: let him be anathema.[23]

THE CODE OF CANON LAW

Canon.849: Baptism, the gateway to the sacraments, is

necessary for salvation, either by actual reception or at least by desire. By it people are freed from sins, are born again as children of God and, made like to Christ by an indelible character, are incorporated into the Church. It is validly conferred only by a washing in real water with the proper form of words.[24]

⊏ 8 ⊐

THE MASS

THE COUNCIL OF TRENT

S ession XXII: Doctrine on the Sacrifice of the Mass

Chapter I: On the Institution of the Most Holy Sacrifice of the Mass

Foreasmuch as, under the former Testament, according to the testimony of the Apostle Paul, there was no perfection, because of the weakness of the Levitical priesthood; there was need, God, the Father of mercies, so ordaining, that another priest should rise, according to the order of Melchisedech, our Lord Jesus Christ, who might consummate, and lead to what is perfect, as many as were to be sanctified. He, therefore, our God and Lord, though he was about to offer himself once on the altar of the cross unto God the Father, by means of his death, there to operate an eternal redemption; nevertheless, because that his priesthood was not to be extinguished by his death, in the Last Supper, on the night in which he was betrayed,—that he might leave, to his own beloved Spouse the Church, *a visible sacrifice, such as the nature of man requires, whereby that bloody sacrifice, once to be accomplished on the cross, might be represented, and the memory thereof remain even unto the end of the world, and its salutary virtue be applied to the remission of those sins which we daily commit,*—declaring himself constituted a priest forever, according to the order of Melchisedech, he offered up to God the Father his own body and blood under the species of bread and wine; and, under the symbols of those same things, he delivered [his own body and blood] to be received by his apostles, whom he then constituted priests of the New Testament; and by those words, Do this in commemoration of me, he commanded them and their successors in the priesthood to offer (them); even as the Catholic Church has always understood and taught.

Chapter II: That the Sacrifice of the Mass is Propitiatory, Both for the Living and the Dead.

For inasmuch as *in this divine sacrifice which is celebrated in the mass is contained and immolated in an unbloody manner the same Christ who once offered himself in a bloody manner on the altar of the cross*; the holy council teaches that *this is truly propitiatory*, and that if we, contrite and penitent, with sincere heart and upright faith, with fear and reverence, draw nigh to God, we obtain mercy and find grace in seasonable aid. For, appeased by this sacrifice, the Lord grants the grace and gift of penitence, and pardons even the gravest crimes and sins. For the victim is one and the same, the same now offering by the ministry of priests who then offered Himself on the cross, the manner alone of offering being different. The fruits of that bloody sacrifice, it is well understood, are received most abundantly through this unbloody one, so far is the latter from derogating in any way from the former. Wherefore, according to the tradition of the Apostles, it is rightly offered not only for the sins, punishments, satisfactions, and other necessities of the faithful who are living, but also for those who are departed in Christ but not as yet fully purified.

Canon I. If any one saith, that in the mass a true and proper sacrifice is not offered to God; or, that to be offered is nothing else but that Christ is given us to eat: let him be anathema.
Canon II. If any one saith, that by those words, *Do this for the*

commemoration of me (Luke xxii. 19), Christ did not institute the apostles priests; or, did not ordain that they and other priests should offer his own body and blood: let him be anathema.

Canon III. If any one saith, that the sacrifice of the mass is only a sacrifice of praise and of thanksgiving; or, that it is a bare commemoration of the sacrifice consummated on the cross, but not a propitiatory sacrifice; or, that it profits him only who receives; and that it ought not to be offered for the living and the dead for sins, pains, satisfactions, and other necessities: let him be anathema.

Canon V. If any one saith, that it is an imposture to celebrate masses in honor of the saints, and for obtaining their intercession with God, as the Church intends: let him be anathema.

Canon VI. If any one saith, that the canon of the mass contains errors, and is therefore to be abrogated: let him be anathema.[25]

THE CATECHISM OF THE COUNCIL OF TRENT

What have we not to hope from the efficacy of a sacrifice in which is immo;lated and offered no less a victim than he, of whom a voice from heaven twice proclaimed: 'This is my beloved Son, in whom I am well pleased.'

The Eucharist was instituted by our Lord for two great purposes, to be the celestial food for our soul, preserving and supporting spiritual life, and to give to the Church a perpetual sacrifice, by which sin may be expiated, and our heavenly Father, whom our crimes have often greviously offended, may be turned from wrath to mercy, from the severity of just vengeanceto the exercise of benignant clemency.

Nor could our divine Lord, when about to offer himself to his eternal Father on the altar of the cross, have given a more illustrious proof of his unbounded love for us, than by bequeathing to us a visible sacrifice, by which the bloody sacrifice, which, a little after, was to be offered once on the cross was to be renewed, and its memory celebrated daily throughout the universal Church even to the consummation of time...

As a sacrament, it is also to the worthy receiver a source of merit...as a sacrifice it is not only a source of merit, but also of satisfaction. As, in his passion, our Lord merited and satisfied for us, so in the oblation of this sacrifice...Christians merit the fruit of his passion, and satisfy for sin.

We, therefore, confess that the sacrifice of the Mass is one and the same sacrifice with that of the cross...That the holy sacrifice of the Mass, therefore, is not only a sacrifice of praise and thanksgiving, or a commemoration of the sacrifice of the cross; but also a sacrifice of propitiation, by which God is appeased and rendered propitious, the pastor will teach as a dogma defined by the unerring authority of a General Council of the Church.[26]

VATICAN II

As often as the sacrifice of the cross in which "Christ, our passover, has been sacrificed" (1 Cor. 5:7) is celebrated on an altar, the work of our redemption is carried on.

In discharging their duty to sanctify their people, pastors should arrange for the celebration of the Eucharistic Sacrifice to be the center and culmination of the whole life of the Christian community.

Through the hands of priests and in the name of the whole Church, the Lord's sacrifice is offered in the Eucharist in an unbloody and sacramental manner until He Himself returns.

Christ is always present in His Church, especially in her liturgical celebrations. He is present in the sacrifice of the Mass, not only in the person of His minister, "the same one now offering, through the ministry of priests, who formerly offered himself on the cross," but especially under the Eucharistic species.

Thus the Eucharistic Action is the very heartbeat of the congregation of the faithful over which the priest presides. So priests must instruct them to offer to God the Father the divine Victim in the sacrifice of the Mass, and to join to it the offering of their own lives.

At the Last Supper, on the night when He was betrayed, *our Savior instituted the Eucharistic Sacrifice of His Body and Blood. He did this in order to perpetuate the sacrifice of the Cross throughout the centuries until He should come again,* and so to intrust to His beloved spouse, the Church, a memorial of His death and resurrection: a sacrament of love, a sign of unity, a bond of charity, a paschal banquet in which Christ is consumed, the mind is filled with grace, and a pledge of future glory is given to us.[27]

THE CODE OF CANON LAW

Canon 897. The eucharistic Sacrifice, the memorial of the death and resurrection of the Lord, in which the Sacrifice of the cross is forever perpetuated, is the summit and the source of all worship and christian life.

Canon 904. Remembering always that in the mystery of the eucharistic Sacrifice the work of redemption is continually being carried out, priests are to celebrate frequently. Indeed, daily celebration is earnestly recommended, because, even if it should not be possible to have the faithful present, it is an action of Christ and of the Church in which priests fulfil their principal role.

Canon 906. A priest may not celebrate the eucharistic Sacrifice without the participation of at least one of the faithful, unless there is a good and reasonable cause for doing so.[28]

THE QUESTION AND ANSWER CATHOLIC CATECHISM

1264. How is the Sacrifice of the Cross continued on earth?

The Sacrifice of the Cross is continued on earth through the Sacrifice of the Mass.

1265. What is the Sacrifice of the Mass?

It is the Sacrifice in which Christ is offered under the species of bread and wine in an unbloody manner. *The Sacrifice of the altar, then, is no mere empty commemoration of the Passion and Death of Jesus Christ, but a true and proper act of sacrifice. Christ, the eternal High Priest, in an unbloody way offers himself a most acceptable Victim to the eternal Father, as he did upon the Cross.*

1269. How does the Mass re-present Calvary?

The Mass re-presents Calvary by continuing Christ's sacrifice of himself to his heavenly Father. In the Mass, no less than on Calvary, Jesus really offers his life to his heavenly Father.

1277. Does the Mass detract from the one, unique Sacrifice of the Cross?

The Mass in no way detracts from the one, unique Sacrifice of the Cross because the Mass is the same Sacrifice as that of the Cross, to continue on earth until the end of time...*The Mass, therefore, no less than the Cross, is expiatory for sins*; but now the expiation is experienced by those for whom, on the Cross, the title of God's mercy had been gained.

1279. How are the merits of Calvary dispensed through the Holy Sacrifice of the Mass?

The merits of Calvary are dispensed through the Mass in that the graces Christ gained for us on the Cross are communicated by the Eucharistic Sacrifice.

1294. Is the Sacrifice of the Mass of infinite value?

The Sacrifice of the Mass is of infinite value, no less than that of the Cross.[29]

CATECHISM OF THE CATHOLIC CHURCH

The Eucharist that Christ institutes...will be the memorial of his sacrifice. Jesus includes the apostles in his own offering and bids them perpetuate it. By doing so, the Lord institutes his apostles as priests of the New Covenant: 'For their sakes I sanctify myself, so that they also may be sanctified in truth'.[30]

Observations: Christ only dies once

These teachings on the Mass are a direct contradiction to the teaching of scripture. According to scripture Christ's death completely dealt with the judgment of God against sin and was *once-for-all* meaning that he could only die once. Christ himself declares that he can never die again (Rev. 1:18). Therefore his death cannot be repeated or in any way perpetuated through time. It can only be memorialized or remembered. Therefore scripture declares that because Christ's death has completely dealt with sin, there are no more sacrifices which are necessary for sin. A sacrifice is propitiatory for sin only if there is a death (Heb. 9:27) and since Christ can only die once, there is only one propitiatory sacrifice, that of the Cross, and it is finished. Scripture teaches that just as Christ's death was *once-for-all,* so the offering of his body and his sacrifice for sin are also *once-for-all* (Heb. 9:26; 10:10) and cannot be repeated or perpetuated through time. It declares that there are no more sacrifices for sin (Heb. 10:18). Therefore, to teach that the Mass is a propitiatory sacrifice for sin because it is the same sacrifice as Calvary is to undermine the teaching of scripture. Since Christ does not die in the sacrifice of the Mass, there can be no true sacrifice for sin. It is not truly propitiatory. And therefore the Mass is not the same sacrifice as Calvary because Christ died at Calvary. To state that the Mass is not an addition to Calvary because it is the same sacrifice would be equivalent to saying, hypothetically, that in the Mass Christ dies but it is not an addition to his death *once-for-all* because it is the same death. Rome utterly repudiates such a notion but only because of the clear statements of scripture. But what Rome fails to understand is that the descriptions of Christ's death and its finality also applies to Christ's sacrifice. Jesus said, 'It is finished.' The teaching of Rome undermines the sufficiency and exclusivity of Christ's atonement and as such undermines the truth of the gospel.

⊐ 9 ⊐

THE PRIESTHOOD

THE COUNCIL OF TRENT

Session XXIII: The True and Catholic Doctrine Concerning the Sacrament of Order

Chapter I: On the Institution of the Priesthood of the New Law.

Sacrifice and priesthood are, by the ordinance of God, in such wise conjoined, as that both have existed in every law. Whereas, therefore, in the New Testament, the Catholic Church has received, from the institution of Christ, the holy visible sacrifice of the Eucharist; it must needs also be confessed, that there is, in that Church, a new, visible, and external priesthood, into which the old has been *translated*. And the sacred Scriptures show, and the tradition of the Catholic Church has always taught, that this priesthood was instituted by the same Lord our Saviour, and that to the Apostles, and their successors in the priesthood, was the power delivered of consecrating, offering, and administering his body and blood, as also of forgiving and of retaining sins.

Chapter I: On the institution of the most holy Sacrifice of the Mass

He, therefore, our God and Lord, though he was about to offer himself once on the altar of the cross unto God the Father, *by means of his death*, there to operate *an eternal redemption*; nevertheless, because that his priesthood was not to be extinguished by his death, in the Last Supper, on the night in which he was betrayed,—that he might leave, to his own beloved Spouse the Church, a visible sacrifice, such as the nature of man requires, whereby that bloody sacrifice, once to be accomplished on the cross, might be represented, and the memory thereof remain even unto the end of the world, and its salutary virtue be applied to the remission of those sins which we daily commit,—declaring himself constituted *a priest forever, according to the order of Melchisedech*, he offered up to God the Father his own body and blood under the species of bread and wine; and, under the symbols of those same things, he delivered [his own body and blood] to be received by his apostles, whom he then constituted priests of the New Testament; and by those words, *Do this in commemoration of me*, he commanded them and their successors in the priesthood to offer [them]; even as the Catholic Church has always understood and taught.

Canon I. If any one saith, that there is not in the New Testament a visible and external priesthood; or, that there is not any power of consecrating and offering the true body and blood of the Lord, and of forgiving and retaining sins, but only an office and bare ministry of preaching the Gospel; or, that those who do not preach are not priests at all: let him be anathema.

Canon III. If any one saith, that order, or sacred ordination, is not truly and properly a sacrament instituted by Christ the Lord; or, that it is a kind of human figment devised by men unskilled in ecclesiastical matters; or, that it is only a kind of rite for choosing ministers of the Word of God and of the sacraments: let him be anathema.

Canon II (On the Sacrifice of the Mass). If any one saith, that by those words, *Do this for the commemoration of me,* (Luke xxii. 19), Christ did not institute the apostles priests; or, did not ordain that they and other priests should offer his own body and blood: let him be anathema.[31]

VATICAN II

Now, the same Lord has established certain ministers among the faithful in order to join them together in one body where "all the members have not the same function" (Rom. 12:4). These ministers in the society of the faithful would be able by the sacred power of their order to offer sacrifice and to remit sins. They would perform their priestly office publicly for men in the name of Christ (p. 534).

Priests are taken from among men and appointed for men in the things which pertain to God, in order to offer gifts and sacrifices for sins...By their vocation and ordination, priests of the New Testament are indeed set apart in a certain sense within the midst of God's people (p. 536)....Priests fulfil their chief duty in the mystery of the Eucharistic Sacrifice. In it the work of our redemption continues to be carried out (p. 560)....The pivotal principle on which the Council's teaching turns is that the priest is a man drawn from the ranks of the People of God to be made, in the very depths of his being, like to Christ, the Priest of mankind. He is consecrated by a special seal of the Holy Spirit. In virtue of this consecration, he acts in the person of Christ, and, as a minister of Christ, the Head, he is deputed to serve the People of God. Through him Christ continues and fulfills that mission which He received from the Father (p. 527).

Therefore, while it indeed presupposes the sacraments of Christian initiation, the sacerdotal office of priests is conferred by that special sacrament through which priests, by the anointing of the Holy Spirit, are marked with a special character and are so configured to Christ the Priest that they can act in the person of Christ the Head (p. 535).[32]

The Code of Canon Law

Canon 900: The only minister who, in the person of Christ, can bring into being the sacrament of the Eucharist, is a validly ordained priest.

CanOn 1008: By divine institution some among Christ's faithful are, through the sacrament of order, marked with an indelible character and are thus constituted sacred ministers; thereby they are consecrated and deputed so that, each according to his own grade, they fulfil, in the person of Christ the Head, the offices of teaching, sanctifying and ruling, and so they nourish the people of God.[33]

Observation:

Roman Catholicism teaches that Christ instituted a sacerdotal priesthood for the express purpose of perpetuating Christ's sacrifice on earth through the Mass. However, scripture teaches that there is no longer a need for a sacerdotal priesthood because there is no more need for sacrifice for sin. Scripture teaches that Christ has fulfilled the office of priest and that such an office has been completely terminated (Heb. 7:11-25).

⊨ 10 ⊨

CONFESSION AND PENANCE

THE COUNCIL OF TRENT

Sixth Session: Decree on Justification; Chapter XIV.

As regards those who, by sin, have fallen from the received grace of Justification, they may be again justified, when, God exciting them, *through the sacrament of Penance* they shall have attained to the recovery, by the merit of Christ, of the grace lost: for this manner of Justification is of the fallen the reparation: which the holy Fathers have aptly called a second plank after the shipwreck of grace lost. *For, on behalf of those who fall into sins after baptism, Christ Jesus instituted the sacrament of Penance,* when he said, Receive ye the Holy Ghost, whose sins you shall forgive, they are forgiven them, and whose sins you shall retain, they are retained. Whence it is to be taught, that the *penitence of a Christian,* after his fall, is very different from that at (his) baptism; and that *therein are included* not only a *cessation from sins,* and a detestation thereof, or, a contrite and humble heart, but also the *sacramental confession of the said sins,*—at least in desire, and to made in its season,—and *sacerdotal absolution*; and likewise *satisfaction by fasts, alms, prayers, and the other pious exercises of the spiritual life*; not indeed for the eternal punishment—

which is, together with the guilt, remitted, either by the sacrament, or by desire of the sacrament—but for the temporal punishment, which, as the sacred writings teach, is not always wholly remitted, as is done in baptism, to those who, ungrateful to the grace of God which they have received, have grieved the Holy Spirit, and have not feared to violate the temple of God. Concerning which penitence is written: Be mindful whence thou art fallen; do penance, and do the first works. And again: The sorrow that is according to God worketh penance steadfast unto salvation. And again: Do penance, and bring forth fruits worthy of penance.

Session XIV: On the Most Holy Sacraments of Penance and Extreme Unction.

Chapter I: On the Necessity, and on the Institution of the Sacrament of Penance.

If such, in all the regenerate, were their gratitude towards God, as that they constantly preserved the justice received in baptism by his bounty and grace, there would not have been need for another sacrament, besides that of baptism itself, to be instituted for the remission of sins. But because God, rich in mercy, knows our frame, he hath bestowed a remedy of life even on those who may, after baptism, have delivered themselves up to the servitude of sin and the power of the devil,—*the sacrament to wit of Penance, by which the benefit of the death of Christ is applied to those who have fallen after baptism*. Penitence was indeed at all times necessary, in order to attain to grace and justice, for all men who had defiled themselves by any mortal sin, even for those who begged to be washed by the sacrament of Baptism: that so, their perverseness renounced and amended, they might, with a hatred of sin and a godly sorrow of mind, detest so great an offense of God. Wherefore the prophet says: Be converted and do penance for all your iniquities, and iniquity shall not be your ruin. The Lord also said: Except you do penance, you shall also likewise perish; and Peter, the prince of the apostles, recommending penitence to sinners who were about to be initiated by baptism, said: Do penance, and be baptized every one of you. Nevertheless, neither before the coming of Christ was penitence a sacrament, nor is it such, since his coming, to any previously to baptism. But the Lord then principally instituted the sacrament of penance, when, being raised from the dead, he breathed upon his disciples, saying: Receive ye the Holy Ghost: whose sins you shall forgive, they are forgiven them, and whose sins you shall retain, they are retained. By which action so signal, and words so clear, the consent of all the Fathers has ever understood that the power of forgiving and retaining sins was communicated to the apostles and their lawful successors, for the reconciling of the faithful who have fallen after baptism. And the Catholic Church with great reason repudiated and condemned as heretics the Novatians, who of old obstinately denied that power of forgiving. Wherefore, this holy Synod, approving of and receiving as most true this meaning of those words of our Lord, condemns the fanciful interpretations of those who, in opposition to the institution of this sacrament, falsely wrest those words to the power of preaching the Word of God, and of announcing the Gospel of Christ.

Chapter III: On the Parts and on the Fruit of this Sacrament.

The holy Synod doth furthermore teach, that the form of the sacrament of Penance, wherein its force principally consists, is placed in those words of the minister: I absolve thee, etc.; to which words indeed certain prayers are, according to the custom of holy Church, laudably joined, which nevertheless by no means regard the essence of that form, neither are they necessary for the administration of the sacrament itself. But the acts of the penitent himself, to wit, contrition, confession, and satisfaction, are as it were the matter of this sacrament. Which acts, inasmuch as they are, by God's institution, required in the penitent for the integrity of the sacrament, and for the full and perfect remission of sins, are for this reason called the parts of penance. But the thing signified indeed, and the effect of this sacrament, as far as regards its force and efficacy, is reconciliation with God, which sometimes, in persons who are pious and who receive this sacrament with devotion, is wont to be followed by peace and serenity of conscience, with exceeding consolation of spirit.

Chapter V: On Confession.

From the institution of the sacrament of Penance, as already explained, the universal Church has always understood that the entire confession of sins was also instituted by the Lord, and is of divine right necessary for all who have fallen after baptism; because that our Lord Jesus Christ, when about to ascend from earth to heaven, left priests his own vicars, as presidents and judges, unto whom all the mortal crimes, into which the faithful of Christ may have fallen, should be carried, in order that, *in accordance with the power of the keys*, they may pronounce the sentence of forgiveness or retention of sins. For it is manifest that priests could not have exercised this judgment without knowledge of the cause; neither indeed could they have observed equity in enjoining punishments, if the said faithful should have declared their sins in general only, and not rather specifically, and one by one. Whence it is gathered that all the mortal sins, of which, after a diligent examination of themselves, they are conscious, must needs be by penitents enumerated in confession, even though those sins be most hidden, and committed only against the last two precepts of the decalogue,—sins which sometimes wound the soul more grievously, and are more dangerous, than those which are committed outwardly. For venial sins, whereby we are not excluded from the grace of God, and into which we fall more frequently, although they be rightly and profitably, and without any presumption, declared in confession, as the custom of pious persons demonstrates, yet may they be omitted without guilt, and be expiated by many other remedies. But, whereas all mortal sins, even those of thought, render men children of wrath, and enemies of God, it is necessary to seek also for the pardon of them all from God, with an open and modest confession.

Chapter VI: On the Ministry of This Sacrament, and on Absolution.

But, as regards the minister of this sacrament, the holy Synod declares all those doctrines to be false, and utterly alien from the truth of the Gospel, which perniciously extend the ministry of the keys to any others soever besides bishops and priests; imagining, contrary to the institution of this sacrament, that those words of our Lord, Whatsoever you shall bind upon earth, shall be bound also in heaven, and whatsoever you shall loose upon earth shall be loosed also in heaven, and, Whose sins you shall forgive, they are forgiven them, and whose sins you shall retain, they are retained, were in such wise addressed to all the faithful of Christ indifferently and indiscriminately, as that everyone has the power of forgiving sins,—public sins to wit by rebuke, provided he that is rebuked shall aquiesce, and secret sins by a voluntary confession made to any individual whatsoever. It also teaches, that even priests, who are in mortal sin, exercise, through the virtue of the Holy Ghost which was bestowed in ordination, the office of forgiving sins, as the ministers of Christ; and that their sentiment is erroneous who contend that this power exists not in bad priests. But although the absolution of the priest is the dispensation of another's bounty, yet is it not a bare ministry only, whether of announcing the Gospel, or of declaring that sins are forgiven, but is after the manner of a judicial act, whereby sentence is pronounced by the priest as by a judge; and therefore the penitent ought so to confide in his own personal faith as to think that,—even though there be no contrition on his part, or no intention on the part of the priest of acting seriously and absolving truly,—he is nevertheless truly and in God's sight absolved, on account of his faith alone.

For neither would faith without penitenance bestow any remission of sins, nor would he be otherwise than most careless of his own salvation, who, knowing that a priest but absolved him in jest, should not carefully seek for another who would act in earnest.

Chapter VIII: On the Necessity and on the Fruit of Satisfaction.

The holy Synod declares, that it is wholly false, and alien from the Word of God, that the guilt is never forgiven by the Lord, without the whole punishment also being therewith pardoned.

And it beseems the divine clemency, that sins be not in such wise pardoned us without any satisfaction, as that, taking occasion therefrom, thinking sins less grievous, we, offering as it were an insult and an outrage to the Holy Ghost, should fall into more grievous sins, treasuring up wrath against the day of wrath. For, doubtless, these satisfactory punishments greatly recall from sin, and check as it were with a bridle, and make penitents more cautious and watchful for the future.

Chapter IX: On Works of Satisfaction.

The Council teaches furthermore, that the liberality of the divine munificence is so great, that we are able through Jesus Christ to make satisfaction to God the Father, not only by punishments voluntarily undertaken by ourselves to atone for sins, or by those imposed by the judgment of the priest according to the measure of our offense, but also, and this is the greatest proof of love, by the temporal afflictions imposed by God, and borne patiently by us.

Canon VI. If any one denieth, either that sacramental confession was instituted, or is necessary to salvation, of divine right; or saith, that the manner of confessing secretly to a priest alone, which the Church hath ever observed from the beginning, and doth observe, is alien from the institution and command of Christ, and is a human invention: let him be anathema.

Canon VII. *If any one saith, that, in the sacrament of Penance, it is not necessary, of divine right, for the remission of sins, to confess all and singular mortal sins* which after due and diligent previous meditation are remembered, even those [mortal sins] which are secret, and those that are opposed to the two last commandments of the Decalogue, as also the circumstances which change the species of a sin; but [saith] that such confession is only useful to instruct and console the penitent, and that it was of old only observed in order to impose a canonical satisfaction; or saith that they, who strive to confess all their sins, wish to leave nothing to the divine mercy to pardon; or, finally, that it is not lawful to confess venial sins; *let him be anathema*.

Canon IX. *If any one saith, that the sacramental absolution of the priest is not a judicial act, but a bare ministry of pronouncing and declaring sins to be forgiven to him who confesses*; provided only he believe himself to be absolved, or [even though] the priest absolve not in earnest, but in jöke; *or saith, that the confession of the penitent is not required, in order that the priest may be able to absolve him: let him be anathema.*

Canon XII. *If any one saith, that God always remits the whole punishment together with the guilt, and that the satisfaction of penitents is no other than the faith whereby they apprehend that Christ has satisfied for them: let him be anathema.*

Canon XIII. *If any one saith, that satisfaction for sins, as to their temporal punishment, is nowise made to God, through the merits of Jesus Christ, by the punishments inflicted by him, and patiently borne, or by those enjoined by the priest, nor even by those voluntarily undertaken, as by fastings, prayers, alms-deeds, or by other works also of piety; and that, therefore, the best penance is merely a new life: let him be anathema.*

Canon XIV. If any one saith, that the satisfactions, by which penitents redeem their sins through Jesus Christ, are not a worship of God, but the traditions of men, which obscure the doctrine of grace, and the true worship of God, and the benefit itself of the death of Christ: let him be anathema.[34]

VATICAN II

Those who approach the sacrament of penance obtain pardon from the mercy of God for offences committed against Him.

By the sacrament of penance sinners are reconciled to God and the Church.[35]

THE CODE OF CANON LAW

Canon 959: In the sacrament of penance the faithful who confess their sins to a lawful minister, are sorry for those sins and have a purpose of amendment, receive from God, through the absolution given by that minister, forgiveness of sins they have committed after baptism, and at the same time they are reconciled with the Church, which by sinning they wounded.

Canon 960: Individual and integral confession and absolution constitute the sole ordinary means by which a member of the faithful who is conscious of grave sin is reconciled with God and with the Church.

Canon 965: Only a priest is the minister of the sacrament of penance.

Canon 966: 1. For the valid absolution of sins, it is required that, in addition to the power of order, the minister has the faculty to exercise that power in respect of the faithful to whom he gives absolution.

       2. A priest can be given this faculty either by the law itself, or by a concession issued by the competent authority in accordance with can. 969.[36]

THE QUESTION AND ANSWER CATHOLIC CATECHISM

1318. What is penance?

Penance means repentance or satisfaction for sin.

1320. Why is the virtue of penance necessary?

The virtue of penance is necessary for a sinner to be reconciled with God. If we expect his forgiveness, we must repent. *Penance is also necessary because we must expiate and make reparation for the punishment which is due for our sins.* That is why Christ tells us, "Unless you repent you will all perish" (Luke 13:5).

1321. What is the sacrament of penance?

Penance is the sacrament instituted by Christ in which sinners are reconciled with God through the absolution of the priest.

1322. Why did Christ institute the sacrament of penance?

Christ instituted this sacrament to give us a ready and assured means of obtaining remission for the sins committed after baptism.

1368. Why is personal, specific confession necessary?

Personal specific confession (called auricular confession) is necessary because this was taught by Christ. He gave his apostles and their successors the power to forgive sins, but also not to forgive them, implying that the faithful had to tell their sins in order for the preist to judge whether they should be absolved.

1386. Why must satisfaction be made for sins already forgiven?

Satisfaction must be made for sins already forgiven because normally some—and even considerable—temporal punishment is still due, although the guilt has been removed.

1392. How can we make satisfactions for our sins?

We make satisfaction for our sins by every good act we perform in the state of grace, but especially by prayer, penance, and the practice of charity. While all prayer merits satisfaction for sin, it is most effective when we ask God to have mercy on us, and unite our prayers with voluntary self-denial. *Penance for sin is not only bodily, like fast and abstinence, but also spiritual, like restraining curiosity or conversation and avoiding otherwise legitimate recreation. Moreover, the patient acceptance of trials or humiliations sent by God is expiatory. Finally, the practice of charity toward others is a powerful satisfaction for our lack of charity toward God.*

1394. What is sacramental satisfaction?

Sacramental satisfaction is the penitential work imposed by a confessor in the confessional in order to make up for the injury done to God and *atone for the temporal punishment due to sin already forgiven. The penitent is obliged to perform the penance imposed by the priest, and deliberate failure to perform a penance imposed for mortal sin is gravely sinful.*

1395. What is extra-sacramental satisfaction?

Extra-sacramental satisfaction is every form of expiation offered to God outside the sacrament of penance. *Our works of satisfaction are meritorious if they are done while in the state of grace and in a spirit of penance.*[37]

CATECHISM OF THE CATHOLIC CHURCH

The interior penance of the Christian can be expressed in many and various ways. Scripture and the Fathers insist above all on three forms, *fasting, prayer,* and *almsgiving,* which express conversion in relation to oneself, to God, and to others. Alongside the radical purification brought about by Baptism or martydom they cite as means of obtaining forgiveness of sins: efforts at reconciliation with one's neighbor, tears of repentance, concern for the salvation of one's neighbor, the intercession of the saints, and the practice of charity 'which covers a multitude of sins (Paragraph #1434, p. 360).

Conversion is accomplished in daily life by gestures of reconciliation, concern for the poor, the exercise and defense of justice and right, by the admission of faults to one's brethren, fraternal correction, revision of life, examination of conscience, spiritual direction, acceptance of suffering, endurance of persecution for the sake of righteousness. Taking up one's cross each day and following Jeus is the surest way of penance.

Eucharist and Penance. Daily conversion and penance find their source and nourishment in the Eucharist, for in it is made present the sacrifice of Christ which has reconciled us with God.

Reading Sacred Scripture, praying the Liturgy of the Hours and the Our Father—every sincere act of worship or devotion revives the spirit of conversion and repentance within us and *contributes to the forgiveness of our sins.*[38]

Observation:

The Roman Catholic Church teaches that an individual can fall from the grace of justification, thereby losing his salvation, and the only means whereby he can regain that grace and a proper standing before God is through the Roman Catholic sacrament of confession and penance. By teaching that men must go through the mediation of a priest to confess sin, that they must receive priestly absolution and that man's works of penance and self-sacrifice expiate sin and are necessary for forgiveness, the Roman Catholic Church undermines the sufficiency of the atonement of Christ. Christ's work of atonement is not sufficient for the attaining of forgiveness. Man's works and sufferings must be added to those of Christ. Such teaching distorts the truth of the gospel.

⌐ 11 ⌐

THE EUCHARIST

THE COUNCIL OF TRENT

Session XIII: Decree Concerning the Most Holy Sacrament of the Eucharist.

Chapter I: On the Real Presence of our Lord Jesus Christ in the Most Holy Sacrament of the Eucharist.

In the first place, the holy Synod teaches, and openly and simply professes, that, in the august sacrament of the holy Eucharist, after the consecration of the bread and wine, our Lord Jesus Christ, true God and man, is truly, really, and substantially contained under the species of those sensible things.

Chapter III: On the Excellency of the Most Holy Eucharist over the Rest of the Sacraments.

And this faith has ever been in the Church of God, that, immediately after the consecration, the veritable body of our Lord, and his veritable blood, together with his soul and divinity, are under the species of bread and wine...Wherefore it is most true, that as much is contained under either species as under both; for Christ whole and entire is under the species of bread, and under any part whatsoever of that species; likewise the whole (Christ) is under the species of wine, and under the parts thereof.

Chapter IV: On Transubstantiation.

And because that Christ, our Redeemer, declared that which he offered under the species of bread to be truly his own body, therefore has it ever been a firm belief in the Church of God, and this holy Synod doth now declare it anew, that, by the consecration of the bread and of the wine, a conversion is made of the whole substance of the bread into the substance of the body of Christ our Lord, and of the whole substance of the wine into the substance of his blood; which conversion is, by the holy Catholic Church, suitably and properly called Transubstantiation.

Chapter V: On the Cult and Veneration to be Shown to This Most Holy sacrament.

Wherefore, there is no room left for doubt, that all the faithful of Christ may, according to the custom ever received in the Catholic Church, render in veneration the worship of latria, which is due to the true God, to this most holy sacrament. For not therefore is it the less to be adored on this account, that it was instituted by Christ, the Lord, in order to be received; for we believe the same God to be present therein, of whom the eternal Father, when introducing him into the world, says: *And let all the angels of God worship him*, whom the Magi, *falling down, adored*; who, in fine, as the Scripture testifies, was adored by the apostles in Galilee.

Canon I. If any one denieth, that, in the sacrament of the most holy Eucharist, are contained truly, really, and substantially, the body and blood together with the soul and divinity of our Lord Jesus Christ, and consequently the whole Christ; but saith that he is only therein as in a sign, or in a figure, or virtue; let him be anathema.

Canon II. If any one saith, that, in the sacred and holy sacrament of the Eucharist, the substance of the bread and wine remains conjointly with the body and blood of our Lord Jesus Christ, and denieth that wonderful and singular conversion of the whole substance of the bread into the body, and of the whole substance of the wine into the blood—the species only of the bread and wine remaining—which conversion indeed the Catholic Church most aptly calls Transubstantiation: let him be anathema.

Canon VI. If any one saith, that, in the holy sacrament of the Eucharist, Christ, the only-begotten Son of God, is not to be adored with the worship, even external of latria; and is, consequently, neither to be venerated with a special festive solemnity, nor to be solemnly borne about in procession, according to the laudable and universal rite and custom of holy Church; or, is not to be proposed publicly to the people to be adored, and that the adorers thereof are idolators: let him be anathema.

Canon VIII. If any one saith, that Christ, given in the Eucharist, is eaten spiritually only, and not also sacramentally and really: let him be anathema[39]

VATICAN II

Christ is always present in His Church, especially in her liturgical celebrations. He is present in the sacrifice of the Mass, not only in the person of His minister, "the same now offering, through the ministry of priests, who formerly offered himself on the cross," but especially under the Eucharistic species (pp. 140-141).

At the Last Supper, on the night when He was betrayed, our Savior instituted the Eucharistic Sacrifice of His Body and

Blood. He did this in order to perpetuate the sacrifice of the Cross throughout the centuries until He should come again (p. 154).

In the house of prayer the most Holy Eucharist is celebrated and preserved. There the faithful gather, and find help and comfort through venerating the presence of the Son of God our Savior, offered for us on the sacrificial altar (p. 543).[40]

The Code of Canon Law

Canon 897: The most venerable sacrament is the blessed Eucharist, in which Christ the Lord himself is contained, offered and received, and by which the Church continually lives and grows. The eucharistic Sacrifice, the memorial of the death and resurrection of the Lord, in which the Sacrifice of the cross is forever perpetuated, is the summit and the source of all worship and christian life.

Canon 898: Christ's faithful are to hold the blessed Eucharist in the highest honour. They should take an active part in the celebration of the most august Sacrifice of the Mass; they should receive the sacrament with great devotion and frequently, and should reverence it with the greatest adoration.

Canon 899: The celebration of the Eucharist is an action of Christ himself and of the Church. In it Christ the Lord, through the ministry of the priest, offers himself, substantially present under the appearances of bread and wine, to God the Father, and gives himself as spiritual nourishment to the faithful who are associated with him in his offering.

Canon 904: Remembering always that in the mystery of the eucharistic Sacrifice the work of redemption is continually being carried out, priests are to celebrate frequently.[41]

THE QUESTION AND ANSWER CATHOLIC CATECHISM

1217. Is the Eucharist necessary for salvation?

The Eucharist is necessary for salvation, to be received either sacramentally or in desire. Christ's words, "if you do not eat the flesh of the Son of Man and drink his blood, you will not have life in you" (John 6:53), mean that Holy Communion is necessary to sustain the life of grace in a person who has reached the age of reason.[42]

⊏ 12 ⊐

Salvation And
The Roman
Church

Pope Boniface VIII (1302 A.D.)

So, when the Greeks and others say that they were not committed to the care of Peter and his successors, they must confess that they are not of Christ's sheep, even as the Lord says in John, 'There is one fold and one shepherd'... Furthermore, that every human creature is subject to the Roman pontiff,—this we declare, say, define, and pronounce to be altogether necessary to salvation.[43]

The Council of Florence

The sacrosanct Roman Church...firmly believes, professes, and proclaims that those not living within the Catholic Church, not only pagans, but also Jews and heretics and schismatics cannot become participants in eternal life, but will depart 'into everlasting fire which was prepared for the devil and his angels' (Matt. 25:41), unless before the end of life the same have been added to the flock; and that the unity of ecclesiastical body is so strong that only to those remaining in it are the sacraments of the Church of benefit for salvation, and do fastings, and almsgiving, and other functions of piety

89

and exercises of Christian service produce eternal reward, and that no one, whatever almsgiving he has practiced, even if he has shed blood for the name of Christ, can be saved, unless he has remained in the bosom and unity of the Catholic Church.[44]

POPE INNOCENT III (1198-1216 A.D.)

By the heart we believe and by the mouth we confess the one Church, not of heretics but the Holy Roman, Catholic, and Apostolic (Church) outside which we believe that no one is saved.[45]

POPE CLEMENT VI (1342-1352 A.D.)

No man of the wayfarers outside the faith of this Church, and outside the obedience of the Pope of Rome, can finally be saved.[46]

PIUS IX (1846-1878 A.D.)

For, it must be held by faith that outside the Apostolic Roman Church, no one can be saved; that this is the only ark of salvation; that he who shall not have entered therein will perish in the flood; but, on the other hand, it is necessary to hold for certain that they who labor in ignorance of the true religion, if this ignorance is invincible, are not stained by any guilt in this matter in the eyes of God...But the Catholic dogma that no one can be saved outside the Catholic Church is well-known; and also that those who are obstinate toward the authority and definitions of the same Church, and who persistently separate themselves from the unity of the Church, and from the Roman Pontiff, the successor of Peter, to whom 'the guardianship of the vine has been entrusted by the Savior,' cannot obtain eternal salvation.[47]

THE COUNCIL OF TRENT

Seventh Session: Decree Concerning the Sacraments

For the completion of the salutary doctrine on Justification...it hath seemed suitable to treat of the most holy Sacraments of the Church, through which all true justice either begins, or being begun is increased, or being lost is repaired. *After this Catholic doctrine on justification, which whosoever does not faithfully and firmly accept cannot be justified.*

Canon I: If anyone saith, that the sacraments of the New Law were not all instituted by Jesus Christ, our Lord; or that they are more, or less, than seven, namely, Baptism, Confirmation, the Eucharist, Penance, Extreme Unction, Order and Matrimony; or that any of these seven is not truly and properly a sacrament: let him be anathema.

Canon IV: *If any one saith, that the sacraments of the New Law are not necessary unto salvation, but superfluous; and that, without them, or without the desire thereof, men obtain of God, through faith alone, the grace of justification;* - though all (the sacraments) are not necessary for every individual: *let him be anathema.*

Canon VIII: *If any one saith,* that by the said sacraments of the New Law grace is not conferred through the act performed, but *that faith alone* in the divine promise *suffices for the obtaining of grace: let him be anathema*[48]

VATICAN I

Further, all those things are to be believed with divine and Catholic faith which are contained in the Word of God, written or handed down, and which the Church, either by a solemn judgment, or by her ordinary and universal magisterium, proposes for belief as having been divinely revealed. And since, without faith, it is impossible to please God, and to attain to the fellowship of his children, therefore without faith no one has ever attained justification, nor will any one obtain eternal life unless he shall have persevered in faith unto the end...The first condition of salvation is to keep the rule of the true faith.

If any one, therefore, shall say that blessed Peter the Apostle was not appointed the Prince of all the Apostles and the visible Head of the whole Church militant; or that the same directly and immediately received from the same our Lord Jesus Christ a primacy of honor only, and not of true and proper jurisdiction: let him be anathema.

If, then, any should deny that it is by institution of Christ the Lord, or by divine right, that blessed Peter should have a perpetual line of successors in the Primacy over the universal Church, or that the Roman Pontiff is the successor of blessed Peter in this primacy: let him be anathema.

We teach and define that it is a dogma divinely revealed: that the Roman Pontiff, when he speaks *ex cathedra*, that is, when in discharge of the office of pastor and doctor of all Christians, by virtue of his supreme Apostolic authority, he defines a doctrine regarding faith and morals to be held by the universal Church, by the divine assistance promised to him in blessed Peter, is possessed of that infallibility with which the divine redeemer willed that his Church should be endowed for defining doctrine regarding faith or morals; and that therefore such definitions of the Roman Pontiff are irreformable of themselves, and not from the consent of the Church. But if any one—which may God avert—presume to contradict this our definition: let him be anathema.

This is the teaching of Catholic truth, from which no one can deviate without loss of faith and salvation.[49]

VATICAN II

This sacred Synod turns its attention first to the Catholic faithful. Basing itself upon sacred Scripture and tradition, it teaches that the Church, now sojourning on earth as an exile, is necessary for salvation. For Christ, made present to us in His body, which is the Church, is the one Mediator and the unique Way of salvation. In explicit terms He Himself affirmed the necessity of faith and baptism (cf. Mk 16:16; Jn.

3:5) and thereby affirmed also the necessity of the Church, for through baptism as through a door men enter the Church. Whosoever, therefore, knowing that the Catholic Church was made necessary by God through Jesus Christ, would refuse to enter her or to remain in her could not be saved.

The mission of the Church concerns the salvation of men, which is to be achieved by belief in Christ and by His grace. Hence the apostolate of the Church and of all her members is primarily designed to manifest Christ's message by words and deeds and to communicate His grace to the world. This work is done mainly through the ministry of the Word and of the sacraments, which are entrusted in a special way to the clergy.[50]

The Question and Answer Catholic Catechism

401. Why did Christ establish the Church?

Christ established the Church as a universal sacrament of salvation.

402. How is the Church the universal sacrament of salvation?

The Church is the universal sacrament of salvation as the divinely instituted means of conferring grace on all the members of the human family.

403. How does the Church communicate divine grace to mankind?

The Church communicates grace to mankind by her teaching of revealed truth, her celebration of Mass and administration of the sacraments, her prayers and the practice of virtue by her members, and her guidance and government of the faithful according to the will of God.

412. Is the Church necessary for salvation?

Yes, the Church is necessary for salvation. Christ himself declared that no one can be saved except through faith and baptism.

413. For whom is there no salvation outside the Church?

There is no salvation for those who, though incorporated into the Church by baptism, fail to persevere in sanctifying grace and die in the state of mortal sin. Those also are not saved who realize what they are doing but refuse to be baptized and accept the Church's means of salvation.

461. What does the Catholic Church believe about the forgiveness of sins?

She believes it is God's will that no one is forgiven except through the merits of Jesus Christ, and that these merits are uniquely channeled through the Church he founded. Consequently, even as the Church is the universal sacrament of salvation, she is also the universal sacrament of reconciliation.

462. How does the Church communicate the merits of Christ's mercy to sinners?

The Church communicates Christ's mercy to sinners through the Mass and the sacraments, and all the prayers and good works of the faithful.

463. What is the Church's role in the reconciliation of sinners to God?

The Church reconciles sinners to God mainly by her exercise of God's mercy, through the sacraments which he instituted.

1119. Are the sacraments necessary for salvation?

According to the way God has willed that we be saved, the sacraments are necessary for salvation.[51]

⊏ 13 ⊐

THE CANON

THE COUNCIL OF TRENT

The holy, ecumenical and general Council of Trent...clearly perceives that these truths and rules are contained in the written books and in the unwritten traditions, which, received by the Apostles from the mouth of Christ Himself, or from the Apostles themselves, the holy Ghost dictating have come down to us, transmitted as it were from hand to hand. Following, then, the examples of the orthodox Fathers, it receives and venerates with a feeling of piety and reverence all the books of both Old and New Testaments, since one God is the author of both; also the traditions, whether they relate to faith or to morals, as having been dictated either orally by Christ or by the Holy Ghost, and preserved in the Catholic Church in unbroken succession. It has thought it proper, moreover, to insert in this decree a list of the sacred books, lest a doubt might arise in the mind of someone as to which are the books recxeived by this council. They are the following: of the Old Testament, the five books of Moses, namely Genesis, Exodus, Leviticus, Numbers, Deuteronomy; Josue, Judges, Ruth, the four books of Kings, two of the Paralipomenon, the first and second of Esdras, the latter of which is called Nehemias, Tobias, Judith, Esther, Job, the Davidic Psalter of 150 Psalms, Proverbs, Ecclesiastes, the Canticle of Canticcles, Wisdom, Ecclesiasticus, Isaias, Jeremias, with Baruch,

Ezechiel, Daniel, the twelve minor Prophets, namely, Osee, Joel, Amos, Abdias, Jonas, Micheas, Nahum, Habacuc, Sophonias, Aggeus, Zacharias, Malachias; two books of Machabees, the first and second.

If anyone does not accept as sacred and canonical the aforesaid books in their entirety and with all their parts, as they have been accustomed to be read in the Catholic Church and as they are contained in the old Latin Vulgate Edition, and knowingly and deliberately rejects the aforesaid traditions, let him be anathema.[52]

⊐ 14 ⊐

PURGATORY

THE COUNCIL OF TRENT

Decree **Concerning Purgatory:** Since the Catholic Church, instructed by the Holy Ghost, has, following the sacred writings and the ancient tradition of the Fathers, taught in sacred councils and very recently in this ecumenical council that there is a purgatory, and that the souls there detained are aided by the suffrages of the faithful and chiefly by the acceptable sacrifice of the altar, the holy council commands the bishops that they strive diligently to the end that the sound doctrine of purgatory, transmitted by the Fathers and sacred councils, be believed and maintained by the faithful of Christ, and to be everywhere taught and preached.

Canons Concerning Justification: Canon 30: If anyone says that after the reception of the grace of justification the guilt is so remitted and the debt of eternal punishment so blotted out to every repentant sinner, that no debt of temporal punishment remains to be discharged either in this world or in purgatory before the gates of heaven can be opened, let him be anathema.[53]

⊐ 15 ⊐

CONCLUSION

In light of the above teachings as officially promulgated by the Roman Catholic Church it is clear that the Church of Rome has defined saving faith in such a way as to undermine its biblical meaning. The Reformers exalted the all sufficiency of the person and work of Christ and the sufficiency and ultimate authority of scripture. All that is necessary to be received and believed relative to salvation is revealed to us in scripture *alone*. However, the Roman Church undermines the authority of scripture by adding dogmas to the deposit of faith which are not only not found in scripture, but which ultimately contradict what is plainly taught there. Its decrees on justification, for example, completely compromise and pervert the gospel as it is clearly presented to us in scripture by defining justification to include the works of sanctification and the sacraments, thereby causing salvation to become a cooperative work between God and man as opposed to a work accomplished once for all by Jesus Christ *alone*. And its teachings not only contradict scripture but are a fundamental denial of the practice and belief of the early Church for one looks in vain for its distinctive teachings on tradition, the papacy, Mary, the canon and purgatory in this early history.

To embrace the ECT call for unity with the Roman Catholic Church means no less than a betrayal of the Lord Jesus Christ himself for such a unity denies the truth of his gospel and the ultimate authority of his word. We must heed the sober word of the apostle Paul:

> I am amazed that you are so quickly deserting Him who called you by the grace of Christ, for a different gospel...But even though we, or an angel from heaven, should preach to you a gospel contrary to that which we have preached to you, let him be accursed. As we have said before, so I say again now, if any man is preaching to you a gospel contrary to that which you received, let him be accursed (Gal. 1:6-9).

On the basis of Rome's own authoritative teachings, there is no basis for unity between the Evangelical and Roman Catholic Churches.

Endnotes

[1]*Dogmatic Decrees of the Vatican Council*, On Faith, Chapter III. Found in Philip Schaff, *The Creeds of Christendom* (New York:Harper, 1877), Volume II, pp. 244-245.

[2]Ludwig Ott, *Fundamentals of Catholic Dogma* (Rockford: Tan, 1974), pp. 4-5, 253.

[3]John Hardon, *The Question and Answer Catholic Catechism* (Garden City: Image, 1981).

[4]*The Canons and Decrees of the Council of Trent*, in Philip Schaff, *The Creeds of Christendom*, Baker Book House (1919 ed.), Seventh Session, *Decree on the Sacraments*, Foreword, pp. 118-119.

[5]*Dogmatic Decrees of the Vatican Council*, Dogmatic Constitution of the Catholic Faith. Found in Philip Schaff, *The Creeds of Christendom* (New York: Harper, 1877), pp. 234-238.

[6]*The Documents of Vatican II* (Chicago: Follett, 1966), Chapter III.18, p. 38.

[7]Philip Schaff, *History of the Christian Church* (Grand Rapids: Eerdmans, 1910), Volume VI, pp. 25-27.

[8]*New Catholic Encyclopedia* (Washington D.C.: Catholic University, 1967), Unam Sanctam, p. 382.

[9]*Dogmatic Decrees of the Vatican Council* as found in *The Creeds of Christendom* by Philip Schaff, Chapters I,II, III.

[10]*Cathechism of the Catholic Church* (New Hope: Urbi et Orbi, 1994), Paragraphs 552-553, 1445, pp. 141-142, 363.

[11]Philip Schaff, *The Creeds of Christendom* (New York: Harper, 1877), Dogmatic Decrees of the Vatican Council, Chp. 4, pp. 266-71.

[12]*The Documents of Vatican II* (Chicago: Follett, 1966), Walter M. Abbott, S.J., General Editor, pp. 47-49.

[13]The Decree of Pope Pius IX on the Immaculate Conception as found in The Creeds of Christendom by Philip Schaff (New York: Harper, 1877), pp. 211-212.

[14]*The Documents of Vatican II* (Chicago: Follett, 1966), Walter M. Abbott, S.J., General Editor, pp. 88, 90.

[15]Selected Documents of Pope Pius XII (Washington: National Catholic Welfare Conference), Munificentissimus Deus 38,40,44-45, 47.

[16]*The Documents of Vatican II* (Chicago: Follett, 1966), Walter M. Abbott, S.J., General Editor, pp. 16, 418, 535, 140-141, 542, 154., pp. 90-91, 94.

[17]Ludwig Ott, *Fundamentals of Catholic Dogma* (Rockford: Tan, 1974), Book Four, Section 2, Chapter I.17, p. 251; Chapter I.18.2-3, p.252-254; Chapter 3.2, p. 264.

[18]*The Canons and Decrees of the Council of Trent*, in Philip Schaff, *The Creeds of Christendom* (Grand Rapids: Baker, 1919 ed.), Decree on Justification, Chapters V, VI, VII, X, XIV, XV, XVI.

[19]*The Canons and Decrees of the Council of Trent*, in Philip Schaff, *The Creeds of Christendom* (Grand Rapids: Baker, 1919 ed.), Seventh Session, *Decree on the Sacraments*, Foreword, pp. 118-119.

[20]*Cathechism of the Catholic Church* (New Hope: Urbi et Orbi, 1994), Paragraphs 1989, 1991-1992, p. 482.

[21]Ludwig Ott, *Fundamentals of Catholic Dogma* (Rockford: Tan, 1974), Book Four, Part I, p.219; 3.5, p. 222; Book III, Part 2, Chapter 2.III.11.3, p. 190; Book IV, Section 2, Chapter 3.23.2, 3.25.1, pp. 264, 267.

[22]John Hardon, *The Question and Answer Catholic Catechism* (Garden City: Image, 1981).

[23]Philip Schaff, *The Creeds of Christendom* (New York: Harper, 1877), Decree on Justification, Chapter IV, p. 91; Canons on Baptism II, V; pp. 122-123.

[24]*The Code of Canon Law* (London: Collins, 1983).

[25]*The Canons and Decrees of the Council of Trent*, in Philip Schaff, *The Creeds of Christendom* (Grand Rapids: Baker, 1919 ed.), pp. 176-180, 184-185.

[26]*The Catechism of the Council of Trent*, Published by Command of Pope Pius the Fifth (New York: Christian Press, 1905), pp. 173-175.

[27]*The Documents of Vatican II* (Chicago: Follett, 1966), Walter M. Abbott, S.J., General Editor, pp. 16, 418, 535, 140-141, 542, 154.

[28]*The Code of Canon Law* (London: Collins, 1983).

[29]John Hardon, *The Question and Answer Catholic Catechism* (Garden: Image, 1981).

[30]*Cathechism of the Catholic Church* (New Hope: Urbi et Orbi, 1994), Paragraph 611, p. 158.

[31]*The Canons and Decrees of the Council of Trent*, in Philip Schaff, *The Creeds of Christendom* (Grand Rapids: Baker, 1919 ed.), pp. 186-187, 191, 184.

[32]*The Documents of Vatican II* (Chicago: Follett, 1966), Walter M. Abbott, S.J., General Editor.

[33]*The Code of Canon Law* (London: Collins, 1983).

[34]*The Canons and Decrees of the Council of Trent*, in Philip Schaff, *The Creeds of Christendom* (Grand Rapids: Baker, 1919 ed.), Decree on Justification, Chapter XIV; Fourteenth Session, On the Most Holy Sacrament of Penance and Extreme Unction, Chapters I, III, V, VI, IX.

[35]*The Documents of Vatican II* (Chicago: Follett, 1966), Walter M. Abbott, S.J., General Editor.

[36]*The Code of Canon Law* (London: Collins, 1983).

[37]John Hardon, *The Question and Answer Catholic Catechism* (Garden: Image, 1981).

[38]*Cathechism of the Catholic Church* (New Hope: Urbi et Orbi, 1994), Paragraph 1435, 1436, 1437, p. 361.

[39]*The Canons and Decrees of the Council of Trent*, in Philip Schaff, *The Creeds of Christendom* (Grand Rapids: Baker, 1919 ed.), pp. 126-131, 136-138.

[40]*The Documents of Vatican II* (Chicago: Follett, 1966), Walter M. Abbott, S.J., General Editor.

[41] *The Code of Canon Law* (London: Collins, 1983).

[42]John Hardon, *The Question and Answer Catholic Catechism* (Garden City: Image, 1981).

[43]From the Bull *Unam Sanctam.* Found in Philip Schaff, *History of the Christian Church* (Grand Rapids: Eerdmans, 1910), Volume VI, pp. 25-27.

[44]Henry Denzinger, *The Sources of Catholic Dogma* (London: Herder, 1954), p. 230, #714.

[45]From the letter *Eius exemplo.* Found in Denzinger, p. 166, #423.

[46]From the letter *Super quibusdum.* Found in Denzinger, p. 204, #570b.

[47]From the Allocution, *Singulari quadem.* Found in Denzinger, pp. 416, 425; #1647, 1677.

[48] *The Canons and Decrees of the Council of Trent*, in Philip Schaff, *The Creeds of Christendom* (Grand Rapids: Baker, 1919 ed.), pp. 118-121.

[49] Philip Schaff, *The Creeds of Christendom* (New York: Harper, 1877), Dogmatic Decrees of the Vatican Council, On Faith, Chapter III; Chp. 4, pp. 266-71.

[50] *The Documents of Vatican II* (Chicago: Follett, 1966), Walter M. Abbott, S.J., General Editor.

[51] John Hardon, *The Question and Answer Catholic Catechism* (Garden: Image, 1981).

[52] *The Canons and Decrees of the Council of Trent*, in Philip Schaff, *The Creeds of Christendom* (Grand Rapids: Baker, 1919 ed.), pp. 17-18.

[53] *The Canons and Decrees of the Council of Trent*, in Philip Schaff, *The Creeds of Christendom* (Grand Rapids: Baker, 1919 ed.), pp. 214, 46.